An Angel
by Your Side

An Angel by Your Side

Finding an angel in your hour of need

Jenny Smedley

CICO BOOKS
LONDON NEW YORK

Published in 2012 by CICO Books
An imprint of Ryland Peters & Small Ltd
20–21 Jockey's Fields
London WC1R 4BW
519 Broadway, 5th Floor
New York, NY 10012

www.cicobooks.com

10 9 8 7 6 5 4 3 2 1

A CIP catalog record for this book is available from the Library of Congress
and the British Library.

ISBN: 978-1-908170-99-6

Printed in China

Illustrator: Trina Dalziel
Editor: Marion Paull
Designer: Ian Midson

For digital editions, visit
www.cicobooks.com/apps.php

"The guardian angels of life fly so high as to be beyond our sight.
But they are always looking down on us."

Jean Paul Richter

CONTENTS

FOREWORD by Jacky Newcomb

We have reached a time in history when angels have stepped forward into the lives of humankind once more. Many of us are experiencing little angel miracles, and believing in angels doesn't seem to be a prerequisite for such happenings. Angels are reaching out to people the world over, regardless of color, age, country of origin, or gender.

I've been working on my own research for many years. Twelve of my thirteen books cover real-life angel experiences to one degree or another, and the demand for them is growing rather than falling away. Internet access has helped spread the word, and social networking sites make it easier than ever to find people who share our interests.

When I first began investigating the angel-experience phenomenon, people would whisper their stories to me. "I've never told anyone this before," they'd say, almost guiltily, or, "I shared this with a close friend and she laughed at me." No wonder people kept quiet about their experiences. Why would you share them with people who didn't appreciate them, or worse, didn't believe you? Over time it has become easier to speak openly about angels. Chatting to a group of people at work, you could mention angels and at least one person would respond positively. It almost became fashionable to believe and the person who had no interest at all became the odd one out!

Celebrities have angels tattooed on their bodies or talk about their own encounters with the other side. Norway's Princess Martha Louise has turned angels into a business, even writing a book *Møt Din Skytsengel* (*Meet Your Guardian Angel.*)

The planet is changing and we are changing with it. Everything, including the planet itself, is raising its vibration. Earth is currently going through a dimensional ascension, a shifting of consciousness. Our knowledge of the Earth and everything around us is growing daily. According to the laws of physics, nothing moves faster than the speed of light, but physicists at Switzerland's CERN laboratory are working to discover particles that do travel faster than light, and if they succeed even in glimpsing them, it will call into question not only Albert Einstein's theory of relativity, but everything we think we know about the world around us. Einstein's theory is central to our understanding of physics and time. So if this is no longer true, does time as we know it even exist? Life, literally, may not be what it seems!

More and more people are coming to the understanding that we are souls living a human existence. Our bodies are "housing" for the soul while we live our earthly life. Earth is just one place that we visit so that our soul can learn and grow. Other planets, worlds, and forms of being do exist and it's time to open our eyes to the truth! The angels have drawn close to help us. It's time to awaken to our place in the universe. Humans are one very small part of the whole. It's common for people to read angel books and remember encounters of their own. "Actually, I remember something like that happened to me once," we'll say. Reading about angels helps with your own awakening, and sharing these experiences helps the spiritual development of others.

Jenny has a unique understanding of these other realms and the changes taking place in our world right now. Her knowledge of angels and all things spiritual will inspire and delight you.

Jacky Newcomb is a bestselling author, *Sunday Times* columnist, and paranormal experiences expert. She is the author of *An Angel Saved My Life* and numerous other bestselling angel and afterlife books.

PREFACE

What are angels and why do we need them in our lives? Angels are known variously as messengers from God or conduits that allow us to connect with God. They're mentioned in all religious tracts in various ways, and have been believed in for thousands of years. To me, angels are my friends and are made of pure energy. In many books you'll read about hierarchies of angels subdivided into archangels and other realms, but I don't like to put angels in "boxes" any more than I like to be labeled and put in a box myself. I just think of angels as divine beings—close to God, yes; able to bring messages from him, yes—but most of all I think of angels as energy sources who operate to help me because they love me. I am not in awe of angels; I love them as much as they love me.

Do you have to have a mind-blowing spiritual experience to know that you've connected with angels? If you don't witness a miracle yourself, does that mean you don't have an angel? No, certainly not. While some people do experience life-changing moments brought about by angels, it doesn't need a miracle of epic proportions to prove to you that angels are on your side. This book has its fair share of stunning true stories of angelic rescue, but it also places focus on the minutiae of angelic signs and interventions that happen every day to ordinary people just like you and me. Start small, and expect small miracles, because in time they will grow into big miracles.

Starting small is important because it will help you to understand how taking notice of the smallest thing in everyday life can lead to you being guided and protected by angels. Be really aware, because angels make use of anything and everything to send messages to their charges. Some events that seem natural in origin can turn out to have been created by angelic invention in order to flag up a response to

something you asked. In times of distress, divine beings can appear in all sorts of guises and be overlooked because of the stress you are going through. It's all down to the timing. If you ask for a sign, expect one and watch for it, even if it comes from an unusual place. Angels can make use of technology, phones, computers, and TVs. They can create signs and signals in everything from clouds to rainbows to iPods. They can even make use of animals and will often send a furry, feathered, or even scaly friend with a message. Life with angels is like following a map. Looking back, you can easily define the turns and paths that led you forward, but when you are looking forward you don't have that gift of hindsight, and so you need a little help to determine the way, and that's where this book comes in.

Accompanying the stories and analysis of them are breathtakingly beautiful illustrations to inspire and uplift you, even in times of deep trouble and energy-sapping sorrow.

When people are depressed, very sad, or even grief-stricken, it's hard to know what to say to bring them solace. This book would be the ideal gift for someone you love and yet don't know how to help.

INTRODUCTION

One of my earliest angel experiences happened years ago when I accidentally ran over a young girl. I had driven my son to school in our big Volvo station wagon (estate car). Having let him out of the car, I was driving on in order to turn around at the bottom of the road, which was a dead-end. I was going slowly, aware of all the children about, and passed a group of girls, chattering and giggling at the curb. As the front of my car passed them, one girl just turned and walked right into it. She was pushed over and vanished in front of the car as she went down. I stood on the brakes and the car stopped almost instantly. The girl started screaming. She screamed and screamed, and I'd never heard such a terrifying sound in my life. I didn't know what to do. My heart was pounding and I was sure my wheel was on top of her, crushing her to death, so my first instinct was to drive forward to get the car off her. But what if I was wrong? What if the car was just on her legs? If I drove forward, I would end up hurting her more seriously as the car would pass over her body. She might have been spun around, so going backward might kill her. Still she screamed. Something told me, "Do not move the car," and I believed it instantly. So I sat there, my feet pressing hard on the clutch and the brake, not daring to move a muscle.

On the other side of the road, the girl's parents had seen what happened. The mother just fell to her knees where she was as she heard her daughter screaming, and started crying, "Oh no, oh God, oh no!" I was still petrified. Luckily, the father found his feet and he ran across the road and fell down on his knees in front of my car, and still I dared not breathe. Suddenly, his head popped up. "Go back, go back," he shouted, flapping his hand at the same time. Gently, I eased the car into reverse, scared it might roll forward, and then even more gently

I released the brake. The car purred back, and, like a miracle, the girl rose to her feet with her dad's arms around her. She was completely unhurt. Her mother ran across to her, touching her from head to foot, unable, like me, to believe she really was all right. Her dad explained that my front wheel had just pinched the edge of her shoe, and the bumper had pushed her to the ground because she couldn't move her foot. She was screaming because her body was right in front of the wheel, while one leg was behind it, and she expected the car to go backward or forward over the top of her at any second while she was trapped there, unable to free her shoe. It had taken her dad just a few seconds to move her around so that I could safely reverse and release the shoe.

Both her parents thanked me profusely for having been going so slowly and being able to stop so quickly. They asked how I'd known to keep the car perfectly still. I didn't know, and that was all I could say. I turned the car around and drove off, but after a couple of miles I had to stop and park, because I was shaking so much. I sat and cried tears of relief and gratitude that my guardian angel, as I now know it was, had guided me that day and saved a child's life. I have a feeling that the little girl's guardian angel was on duty too. I can only imagine how different and troubled the rest of my life might have been if I'd been responsible for killing or seriously injuring a child.

Another time I was out in the countryside with some friends and we got caught in a sudden, violent, summer thunderstorm. Never, before or since, have I heard such thunder or seen such spectacular lightning. It was doubly terrifying because we were out in the open with only trees for shelter. Of course, standing under a tree is the worst place to be in an electrical storm because lightning is drawn to tall objects, especially when they stand out on otherwise flat ground, as the trees did on that day. We were all huddled together, a group of young teenagers, wondering what to do for the best, when someone spotted a light, flickering through the sheets of rain, glowing like a beacon in the lowering, cloud-induced darkness. We staggered through the long, wet grass, soaked to the skin, not able to hear each other speak in the drumming of the rain and the crashing of the thunder. It was a wooden cottage, well more of a shack really, but when it loomed out of the murk, we couldn't have been more delighted if it had been a palace. A figure in the open doorway was silhouetted by the light from within. We couldn't see, and didn't care, who it was as we piled past the beckoning arms into the warmth of the cottage. Once inside and with the door shut, we realized that the figure was an elderly man, swathed in shawls. His pants were held up with string. He had a straggly, gray beard, and to us youngsters looked at least 100 years old, although in hindsight I'm sure he wasn't as old as that. None of us can remember

much apart from sitting in a row on a rough-carved wooden bench and being handed mugs of steaming tea that he had brewed on a small bottled-gas hotplate. Time passed in a haze and soon so did the storm, and we went on our way.

The next day a few of us couldn't recall saying thank you to the old man, although we couldn't be sure, and we felt really guilty—so guilty that we decided we had to go back. We took him a present. I can't recall what it was, but that's not important, because no matter how many times we crossed and re-crossed the fields and woods, we couldn't find the shack. It was just as if it and our savior had never existed.

I realized early on that I had a connection to angels—right from the time a pair of unseen hands caught me when, as a young child, I jumped from a train pulling out of a station—and I've dedicated most of my time to getting even closer to them, and trying to help other people to do the same. No matter what troubles you have, and no matter what grief and worries you're trying to deal with, the presence of an angel at your side can forge miraculous changes, even if angels can't solve all of your problems. For instance, although they can't bring back a loved one who has passed on, they can help you cope with it. For a start, the sensation of love you get when your angel is near is incomparable, and can sustain you through most things. Also, an angel can help your passed-over loved one send you a message, which may be huge and obvious, or small and seemingly insignificant to anyone else.

We all have our problems. No one's life is perfect, and we're all here to learn lessons, so there are some things that we just have to endure. But with the help of angels we'll find our strength returning. They really are all around us all the time. We just need to make that connection and life will feel better. To know there are angels automatically means we know there is life after death, and this, too, is a huge comfort.

The worst state to be in is when it seems like we're just being carted along as part of life's flotsam, at the mercy of some faceless and unfeeling destiny. With the help of angels, we're able to see that there is order in the universe, and that we're *taking part* in events rather than just having them happen to us. A soul angel helped me when I needed it most, by causing me to recall a past life. The understanding that I had lived before helped me to know why I'm here this time around, and gave me a sense of purpose. The fulfillment that comes from achieving, or even working toward the purpose, is the secret to inner happiness.

I was on a train, of all places, when my most dramatic encounter with an angel happened. I was suddenly in another place with a glowing golden being towering over me. The only emotion I felt at the time was overwhelming love, both given and received in equal measure. This angel, and I only came to realize later that's what it was, showed me my path very clearly. I was to become a "seed planter"—I was to plant a seed of spirituality in as many people as I could. It didn't matter whether this was the idea of past lives, angels, the immortality of souls, or our connectedness with the planet. Any seed that caused someone to think out of the rat-race box would do. In order to achieve my mission, I was given certain tools, which I'll talk more about later.

Different angels can help in different ways. I don't tend to categorize them, because I think they are mostly multipurpose, or give them names, because I don't think they need or use them. Angels recognize us and each other simply by the energy that is projected. They allow us to give them names if we feel the need, just to make it easier for us, because we've lost the ability to see and feel energy to a large extent. Once we reconnect with our angels, though, we start to regain this ability. When we need angelic help, we don't need to call out to an angel by name, or select one that fits the job description. We just need to open our hearts and the right angel will come to us. The hardest element to get right in this is to trust. That's such a big word—when everything seems hopeless, trusting is the hardest thing in the world to do. But, if we can succeed in this, we will be rewarded.

CHAPTER 1

SAVED BY AN ANGEL

Sometimes angels will create what appears to be an annoying delay in your life. For instance, one day my husband Tony and I were leaving the house to drive to a meeting, and after we'd gone about half a mile I realized I'd left my briefcase behind. I couldn't understand how I'd come to forget it. I'd left it right by the door so that I'd virtually trip over it on the way out. We went back for it and, to my astonishment, the briefcase was on the bed in our bedroom. It was irritating having to backtrack, but we set off again and a couple of miles on found ourselves in a line of stationary cars. There had been a multiple accident ahead. Needless to say, we were very grateful to whatever angel had chosen to make us late that day!

So, whenever life appears to be throwing you a curve ball, and you don't end up where you expected to be when you expected to be there, just pause for a moment and ask yourself whether this delay was actually meant to be. Who knows what disasters you might be guided to avoid in this way? Acceptance of a seemingly annoying redirection can enhance your general connection to your angels, because angels find it easier to interact with your energy when you are calm.

Robin's story:

Brotherly Love

My brother, Mark, died on April 9, 2003, just eighteen days after I gave birth to my first child. Of course, it was devastating to lose my brother, and especially to have to deal with the grief and loss at a time that should have been nothing but joyous for my entire family. As it was, none of them could give me any kind of emotional support, because they were all lost in grief themselves. Maybe it was because of this that I started recognizing that my brother was in fact still with me only hours after he'd crossed over. But it was only later, after I'd read a book by Patrick Mathews, who is a gifted medium, that I was really able to understand my brother's connections with me.

On the first anniversary of Mark's death, my husband Andy, our one-year-old son, and I were visiting Carmel and Pacific Grove, California. We'd gone there for the day from our home in San José. We told ourselves to be on the lookout for signs from Mark, because we'd read about such things occurring in the book, and we knew he was with us. We saw the odd random hawk, but nothing extraordinary. And then it happened.

It was late that afternoon, and I was driving us north toward Santa Cruz. There had been a lot of traffic for the whole journey, but when I glanced in my rearview mirror suddenly there were no other cars in sight, except a black SUV, which was right behind me, about 20 feet away. I looked away and that's when I heard this scraping, banging, horrifying noise, like a flatbed truck driving fast over a lot of bumps or a steel bridge. I asked Andy, "Did you hear that?" The SUV flipped

Lucky escapes

Tony and I had been dating for a few months when we escaped an apparently certain head-on collision with an overtaking oil tanker that was coming right at us. Although we were on a major highway, back in those days it was just two carriageways wide. Coming toward us was a long line of traffic, headed by a slow-moving tractor. It must have been very frustrating for the drivers following it and that must have been what made the driver of an oil tanker from the nearby refinery make a reckless move to overtake it. When we saw the tanker cresting the brow of the hill on our side of the road, I think we both thought it was all over. There was nowhere for us to go, and by the time the driver saw us, he was alongside the tractor, and he had nowhere to go, either. At the last possible split second, when we could practically see the whites of the tanker driver's eyes, a gap opened to our left where a busstop had been created. Tony was able to swerve our car out of harm's way, and then back onto the carriageway, with a fraction of an inch to spare.

Another time, a crashing car somersaulted toward us. It should have hit us, but it was suddenly halted in midair by an apparently invisible barrier, and it crashed to the road, feet from the front of our car. We have also lost a wheel just seconds after turning onto a quiet lane off a busy highway, where we'd been traveling at speed.

over, landed upside down, and slid across the highway I was moving at 55mph, in the fast lane, so the distance between us increased quickly—we were the only car ahead of the spot where the SUV landed. I saw it crash to the ground as if in slow motion. I said a prayer for the people in the vehicle, and, of course, we were very shaken up.

When we resumed our journey to Santa Cruz, we were discussing how we believed Mark had either caused us to make changes to what we were doing so that our timing didn't coincide with the accident, or that he'd used his angel power to push us further up the highway and move us out of reach of the crash. It was surreal, because we missed a fatal collision by so little, and whatever the case we thanked Mark and God for providing us with that barrier.

As if in confirmation, later, when I took a picture at Lake Table of my husband and son, and uploaded it, my brother's face was depicted in the clouds. It blew me away. I was so surprised. It was as if he'd pushed his face into the veil in order to reach out to us.

Jenny says:

I've been sent dozens of stories like this one, and Tony and I have been saved from several possibly fatal road accidents, often in ways that have seemed to be totally miraculous. I'm often asked, if people can be saved, why isn't everyone saved? The answer is that we all have our own paths to walk, and sometimes it's just time to leave. Angels can divert disasters only if they don't comply with the predetermined plans for that person. Our souls are constantly evolving, and in order to do so they have to encounter adversity from time to time. Sometimes they have to leave this world for their own higher good and the progress of their souls, impossibly hard to accept though it is for those left behind.

Cindhi's story:

Balancing Act

As a teenager I liked to go to rodeos. One time, I was stupidly and overconfidently sitting on the wooden back gate, which was topped with loose wires, when a bull rider fell off right in front of me. The big bull looked me in the eye, then ran straight toward me and slammed into the gate. The gate flew backward and forward and before I knew

it I was looking down at his wide, pointed horns while hanging on to the wires for dear life. The clowns, who are there to distract the bull when someone falls off, tried to get him away from me, but

Jenny says: It's a funny thing that when something inexplicable happens right in front of your eyes, you can sometimes just allow your mind to skip over it, without it impacting on you, which is what happened with the people who witnessed Cindhi's bizarre balancing act. If the brain can't process what the eyes are seeing in a logical way, it just ignores it. So, if something does happen in front of you, force your logical left brain to switch off for a moment, and allow your intuitive right brain to capture and digest the moment.

he wasn't interested. I started to lose my grip and fall, and I really thought I was going to go under his hooves. Then somebody took me around the waist from behind, and steadied me until I regained my balance and the bull finally moved away. I was so relieved that I immediately turned around to say thank you to the person who had saved me, but there was no one, I mean no one, even close to me. I got down from the gate and ran around to ask people if they'd seen anyone, and they just laughed at me for flopping around so wildly. They all thought they saw me regain my balance by myself.

The numbers game

It's a good idea to keep a diary of mystifying events as they occur, because once you start to accept them, it seems that you will have more and more of them to process. Little signs and interventions that happen every day can often be misread or even ignored. For instance, some people's angels send them indications of their presence with repetitively occurring numbers. A very common one is 11:11. So if you keep seeing the same number on clocks, number plates, digital readouts, or anything else, then the chances are your angel is trying to tell you something. Sometimes this can be worked out through the science of numerology—11:11 reduces to the number 4 (1 + 1 + 1 + 1 = 4) and 4 is the recognized number of the everlasting friend, which is of course what your angel is to you.

Gill's story:

Warning Sign

I had just left the supermarket with my groceries, and was headed for home. The road I was driving on has a 40mph speed limit, which I was reaching when a car coming the other way flashed its lights at me. I presumed the driver was trying to warn me about police doing speed checks, so I slowed down, although I wasn't speeding. A split second later, ladders on the roof of a van coming toward me broke loose and flew off. Had I not been flashed at and so slowed down, those ladders would definitely have come through the windscreen of my car and probably killed me. The amazing thing is I start a job at the same supermarket tomorrow, and I've been asking the angels for a sign to let me know I'll be happy there. I take being lucky to escape a bad accident as a sign. I was also lucky to get the job in the first place, because I'm not qualified for it. I had been asking for financial help.

Jenny says: It seems that Gill's angels gave her a double whammy here, answering her question and saving her life at the same time. Of course, the other car driver might have flashed her without angelic help, but would Gill have listened, especially as she wasn't going too fast anyway? Possibly not, and this is where the left brain needs to be switched off and the sign accepted if you want to get closer to your angels, as Gill did.

Angel aid

It's a very good idea to summon angelic protection for yourself and your family every day. A simple process of vizualization will soon become second nature—the more you do it, the quicker it becomes. It really doesn't matter what you choose to visualize. The important thing is the intent to create protection and you just do it in whatever way you find easiest. Here are some suggestions.

* Picture a column of white light descending over you from heaven.
* Picture yourself dressed in a silver suit, like a spaceman.
* Picture a dome of gold enveloping you.
* Picture a dome of white or gold light over your car to protect you from accidents and from the road rage of other drivers. If you do this and someone starts tail-gating you, just push your dome of light toward the offending car and the driver will back off.

Lynn's story:

Look Twice

Eight years ago, my mother and grandmother, with whom I lived, were away visiting family, and so I asked my friend Jayne to stay. One day she said she was popping home for a couple of hours. As she was standing in the living-room doorway, chatting away, a wispy figure appeared behind her. I immediately knew it was her guardian angel and I heard a soft voice say, "Keep her talking, and tell her to be careful crossing the road." I passed on the message and that started Jayne talking again.

The angel was a little mischievous, and began mimicking Jayne. That made me smile, and Jayne wanted to know why I was smiling. So I told her about the angel, and what it was doing, but she couldn't see anything. I said, "Just take the angelic advice anyway, and be careful." Jayne said she would.

She left shortly after that and later rang me from her place. She told me that when she'd reached the traffic lights at the end of the village where we live, the green man was showing, which should have meant it was safe for pedestrians to cross. But just as she was about to step into the road, she remembered the warning, and didn't walk across, but paused for another look. Straightaway a motorcycle came speeding around the corner, right through the red light. If Jayne had been crossing the road, the motorcycle would have hit her. If the angel hadn't visited us to warn her, Jayne wouldn't be here today. Since that day I always ask the angels to look after all of my family and friends. And I know that they do.

Jenny says: This kind of thing happens a lot. In fact it happened to me the other day. I was crossing the road to go to the meditation group I co-run, and I thought the road was clear. I took one step and in my mind had already taken the next, leaning into it, when something pulled me up in midair and held me back as a car suddenly whizzed round the corner. The car missed me by a few inches. Then, as my weight was already tipped forward, I should have slammed into the side of the passing car, but I was still held, just far enough back to stop me falling until the car had gone past. If you get a warning or get helped like this, don't question it. After all, this is what guardian angels are here for!

Michelle's story:

Help from a Stranger

My first experience of angels was when I was saved in a car accident in New Zealand, at the age of sixteen. I was with a boyfriend and two of his mates, and to this day I'm not really sure what happened to make the car slide out of control. It suddenly spun dizzily, and turned on its side, and finally slid to a stop about a foot away from a streetlight. All of us were okay. I had the worst bruises, but the amazing thing was how I got out of the two-door car. To start with, I was in the back seat where there were no doors, and must somehow have climbed into the front. One side of the car was against the road surface, so the only way out was through the other doors, which were now above my head. Being small (5ft 2in.), I could not lever myself out of the car without help. We were on a relatively remote road and nobody else was around, but a really lovely man came running up from nowhere, calling my name, and he helped me get out of the car. At the time, the fact that he knew my name didn't register. By the time I got my head together and turned to thank him, he was gone. No one else saw him, and the others thought I had gone into shock, but there was no way I could have got out of that car by myself. I put it down to him being my guardian angel. I know I have been, and am always being, looked after.

Jenny says:

Although Michelle's helper was invisible to others, you sometimes read of real people being temporarily imbued with extraordinary strength. My brother was once in a frozen food shop, when a chest freezer full of food fell off its stand onto a child. Without thinking my brother lifted the very heavy chest off the child, yet minutes later he was unable to budge it. Sometimes people are able to wrench off jammed car doors, or right overturned cars with strength they don't usually possess. I'm sure that science could come up with some natural reason for this, but to me the reason is simple: they had divine help.

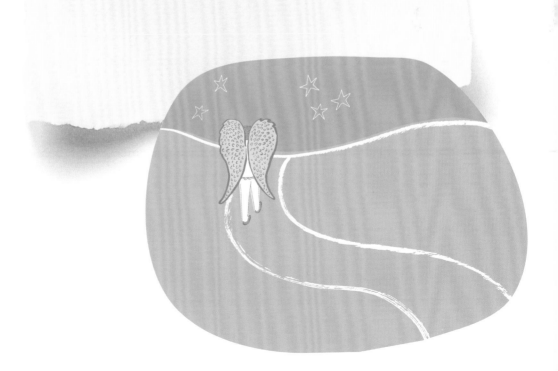

William's story:

"Someone's Lookin' out for You"

I was a teenager just learning how to drive, and was out in the car with some friends late one night in northeastern Oregon. We were on a gravel country road in the dark, and I was going way too fast. I forgot the road took a sharp turn ahead and as I hit the corner, the car began fishtailing all over the place. The ditches on either side of the road were at least eight feet deep and I tried desperately to avoid them. Well, the car stayed on the road somehow. My friends said that it was good driving skill, but the nearmiss wouldn't have happened at all if my driving skill had been any good in the first place.

The next day I was at my job as a cashier at a local gas station, relating the previous night's driving events to one of my coworkers, when an older woman, dressed in some of the most mismatched pieces of clothing I've ever seen, approached to pay for her gas. She had been listening in on my conversation, I guess. When I put her change on the counter, she commented, "Someone's lookin' out for you," and then she turned and went out through the front doors, leaving her change where it was. I quickly grabbed it and headed out of the door after her. I was no more than two seconds behind but the only person in the front of the gas station was a man on a motorcycle. I checked the two other sides of the station to see if she had somehow pulled around or parked off to one side. Nothing. She'd seemingly disappeared. I still remember to this day the feeling of strange but wonderful awe that I felt after this event. It was definitely one of the odder things that has happened to me in my life.

Jenny says: You never know when an angel might enter your life, because they can appear in many forms—a column of light, a handsome young man or a beautiful girl, an ancient crone or an old man. They can even show themselves as animals. I once met a young girl who saw her angel as a unicorn. The moral of this story is never to say a harsh word to a stranger without due cause, and be aware of the effect that simple words can have on you and those around you. Choose your words and actions carefully, because you never really know in whose company you might be. And, of course, if you accept and recognize the incident for what it really is, the knowledge can bring you solace whenever you need it throughout your life.

Entertaining angels unawares

Sometimes I think these appearances are a test of sorts. For instance, you might be asked for help by someone you wouldn't normally think of helping. Of course, I'm not advocating stopping to pick up some strange hitchhiker on the road when you're alone and it's dark—angels would never want you to take that sort of risk. But if you pass someone on the street who is really struggling in some way, maybe see if there's something you can do for them, because you never know who they might really be. If someone calls at your house asking for directions, as happened to me, and he's elderly and obviously tired, think about perhaps letting him rest or giving him a drink before you send him on his way, as well as helping with the directions.

CHAPTER 2

VISITED BY AN ANGEL

Many stories come from people who believe they met an angel in times of trouble, sometimes at a loved one's sick bed. Hospitals are often visited by angels. They seem to bring messages of hope to those who wouldn't perhaps be able to continue down their rightful path without it. Hospitals have a very strange atmosphere all of their own, which isn't surprising, and some people find it hard to cope with them. The silver lining is that they are good places to receive signs from angels. I think this is because those people needing angelic help are often in a "confined" state of mind. By this I mean that they are totally switched off from the real world and are isolated in the rarefied energy of the hospital. I've had many letters and emails over the years from nurses, and most of them admit to having seen some very strange sights while nursing extremely ill patients.

Dawn's story:

Angel of Hope

I gave birth to my son Quinn on August 6, 2000 at about 4 a.m. Tragically, he was premature and didn't survive. I was alone and crying in the hospital room when a woman walked in. She was about five feet tall, with dark curly hair, and not very attractive—her facial features seemed too big for her face. She wasn't wearing a hospital uniform, and had no nametag. She walked over, hugged me, and said very gently, "Don't cry. You're going to be okay. Do you understand me? You're going to be okay." I nodded and thanked her, and as she left the room, I finally stopped crying.

Five minutes later a nurse came in to check me, and I asked her who the woman was. She had no idea what I was talking about, and told me that only medical professionals were around the wards at that hour. She looked very puzzled. I wasn't sedated or medicated in any way but I knew the strange woman was real. At the time it never crossed my mind that she was an angel. The grief of having just lost my son overrode all other thoughts and emotions. It wasn't until about two years later, when I encountered the same woman again, that I knew.

I was at a workshop and, during one of the exercises, I found myself telling the story of my son Quinn, and his death, the first time I'd spoken of it since it happened. That night, back in my hotel room, I lay on my side on the bed, with my back to the door, the events of the day running through my mind. Suddenly, the room lit up from behind me and I thought someone had come in, but I knew without doubt that the door was locked. I couldn't move. I was literally paralyzed. I lay there on my side, eyes wide open, breathing heavily, scared, and completely unable to move. The edge of the bed behind my back sunk

as someone sat down, and a body leaned against me. The person bent down close to me and a woman's arm passed in front of my eyes as she put her hand on the bed to support herself. Long, dark, curly hair brushed my face, and she put her mouth up to my ear.

"Hi," she whispered. I actually felt her breath on my ear. I didn't see her face, but I knew immediately it was the woman from the hospital two years before. Somehow I managed to whisper, "Hi," back.

Then she left, and light filled the room as it had when she'd come in. I could move again, but I didn't know what to do. I thought of calling the front desk, but what would I tell them? A strange woman came into my room, said hi, and then left? I sat up for hours, trying to make sense of it all. That's when I came to the conclusion that she was an angel, and that she reappeared because I'd told the story of Quinn, which I'd never done before. I haven't seen her since, but I really wish she'd come back, so maybe I could ask her a question or two.

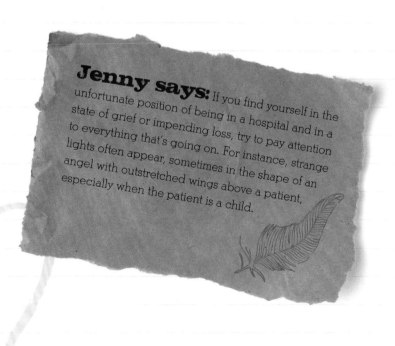

Jenny says: If you find yourself in the unfortunate position of being in a hospital and in a state of grief or impending loss, try to pay attention to everything that's going on. For instance, strange lights often appear, sometimes in the shape of an angel with outstretched wings above a patient, especially when the patient is a child.

Lisa's story:

Cometh the Hour

In 2001 my maternal grandma was dying of cancer. Originally, she was given a couple of months to live, but she lived for another year. My grandma was a fiery, red-haired Leo and the matriarch of our family. She was my best friend, and had really played a role in raising me. It was hard to see her dying. She refused a hospice, but the hospital was kind enough to allow us to be in her room night and day. During the last week of her life, she was in a morphine-induced coma of sorts to manage her pain.

I was attending massage school at the time, finishing up my clinicals, but I spent as much time with her as I could. After class one morning, I knew that my grandma was going to pass. When I arrived at the hospital room, my grandpa was there, along with some relatives. A blond-haired woman wearing a white pantsuit came into the room. She said she was a hospital lay minister and asked if we wanted to say a prayer. We agreed, even though we're not a very religious family. It just felt so good to be in this lay minister's energy. She was so sweet and loving. Shortly afterward, I was alone with my grandma, and I talked to her telepathically—I'd always been psychic and I shared that with my grandma. I said that I understood why she had to leave and that I loved her. I told her I didn't want her to suffer and that I was sure that we'd connect once she had transitioned over to the other side. It hurt me to let her go, but I just did my best. My grandma passed away at a little after 11 p.m. My watch stopped at that time. At least three people have since tried to repair it, but couldn't. I cried, of course, but I wanted to be strong for my family, and so I put my grief on hold until later, when I was done with school, which is not always the best way to deal with things.

I wanted to thank everyone at the hospital for their kindness, and spoke to my grandma's nurses, who had been so compassionate. I also wanted to deliver a note of thanks to the lay minister who came to pray with us. So I went to the spiritual support office at the hospital to find out her name. The woman at the desk said no such woman worked for them or visited as a volunteer. All volunteers, she said, had to check in with the hospital first. I thought it was odd and I'm sure she did! But, in hindsight, I really believe this lay minister was an angel.

Later, when I studied angels in more depth, I learned that sometimes the Divine sends us earth angels to help us in our time of need. I was so upset at the time of my grandma's death and had no idea how to let her go. I really believe in my heart that the divine sent me an angel in the form of the lay minister. I write this about six days from the tenth anniversary of my grandma's death. I don't think that this is a coincidence at all!

Jenny says:

Expect angels every day. I've heard and read many versions of this story over the years. It really does seem that angels will visit families at their loved one's deathbed. The stories come from all kinds of people from all walks of life. There are too many and they are too similar not to be true. If you find yourself in this situation, as we all do sometimes, pay attention to those who come to help or bring words of comfort. In times of huge distress it's easy to overlook or forget about them, but if you come to understand that you've been given angelic help, this will comfort you, not just at the time but for the rest of your life.

Simon's story:

Angel of Kindness

I was very close to my grandpa, and when he was in hospital I spent as much time with him as I could, knowing there wasn't much time left. One evening, I was totally shattered and fell asleep in the chair across the room from the bed. I don't know if I was dreaming, but I saw a

being with wings in front of me. Then, and I don't understand why I would have dreamed this, because as far as I knew my grandpa was still with me, this being took my hand and led me to the bed. As we got there, the being took my grandpa's hand, too. He had been unconscious and unable to move for days, but he sat up and the being placed our hands together. We clasped hands and then hugged. My grandpa whispered, "Goodbye, I love you," and then he stopped breathing. I woke up, still in the chair, and looked across, knowing what I would see. All the machines had flat-lined and grandpa was gone. The doctors rushed in and worked on him, but I knew he had gone. I'm very grateful that the angel, for that was what it must have been, came and allowed me to say goodbye, otherwise I would have missed the moment.

Ready to go

This is very similar to what happened to me when my dad passed away. He was under sedation and on morphine and couldn't move, yet I saw his spirit rise up from his body, and stand, just attached by the feet. He sort of tugged, like a helium-filled tethered balloon, as if trying to escape his earthly body, but he was stuck and couldn't manage to detach. This image filled me with comfort because it proved that he not only wanted and was ready to go, but that he also had somewhere to go, and couldn't wait to get there! When he did finally breathe his last a few hours later, there was a flash of gold as his soul exited through the window and shot upward to freedom.

Terry's story:

Never Give Up

My name is Terry Grahl, and I'm the founder and visionary of Enchanted Makeovers. I'm also a wife, mother to four wonderful children, storyteller, activist, author, interior decorator, and a passionate woman on a mission to inspire people to dream while they are awake, follow their heart, and most importantly, to see each other truly as an extension of one's self.

I've been on one amazing journey since 2007, but in 2008 I was ready to give up, not only on myself but on women and children living in shelters. In March 2008 I was working on one particular shelter, attempting to transform the space for those living there. The months before that had been extremely hard with no donations arriving and the volunteers not understanding the importance of doing a great job, and what it says about ourselves when we slack. As I was leaving the shelter one day, I broke down and began to cry to the director. In the hallway I said to her, "Why don't they get it? Why don't they see that the women and children deserve better?"

Then I heard a soft voice say, "They need to treat it like God's home." A woman who did not live at the shelter, and who was not sitting in the hallway when I first came in, was right there in front of me. She looked like a bag lady you would see in a movie, with the black trench coat, boots, and an old holdall. I was in awe, and in my heart felt that she was an angel who had been sent to urge me, "Don't give up! Keep moving forward!"

Jenny says: It's obviously Terry's path to do the wonderful work she's doing, and her angels would have seen that she was about to slip from it. So one of them appeared just to her in order to renew her faith and passion for her life's work.

I called the shelter as soon as I got home and what still amazes me is that when I mentioned the odd visitor, the director said, "What woman? There was no woman in the hallway." I'm so glad I never gave up, because today Enchanted Makeovers is an award-winning, non-profit-making organization, which is recognized internationally.

Check you are on the right path

Really, there's quite a simple way to recognize this. If you ever feel like giving up on something, ask for a sign and watch out for a message. If you don't get one, the odds are that you're not currently on your life's rightful path and perhaps you need to take a step back and re-evaluate what you're doing. It's been proven to me over and over again that when we are going the right way, doors open rather than close, and little miracles constantly occur to keep our faith strong. If you do see another way, take a baby step toward it in total trust, because if you're right, you will get help to move forward.

Jasmine's story:

Gypsy Fortune

We live in Canada, in a beautiful place. Across the road from us is a mountain lake. The view is gorgeous, but I've always been aware that large bodies of water and young children don't mix, so our house and garden are very secure for our four-year-old son. You can imagine my shock when I looked out of the window one day and saw him standing by the edge of the lake, talking to a strange woman. She looked a little like you might imagine a Romany woman to look, with really colorful clothes and a headscarf.

Naturally, I rushed out of the house and across the street in a flash, yelling at the woman to leave my son alone. Straightaway I realized that I should be grateful to her, because she'd stopped him from falling in the water, but how did he get out? Did she let him out? Was she trying to take him? As I got there, I saw that her scarf was beaded with sparkling crystals, and something about her made me calm right down. She looked at me from bright blue eyes, half hidden behind curly black hair. I found myself on my knees beside my son. Later, we discovered that he had found a way to climb the garden wall and had got out by himself, but at the time, I don't know why, I suddenly knew he was safe with this woman. I picked him up and hugged him, half scolding him and half telling him mommy loved him.

Once I'd got my breath back, I turned to the woman to thank her, but she'd gone. I have to tell you that we live in a small isolated settlement and no one, especially someone like her, could have been in the area without being noticed, but I never saw her again, and no one else had ever seen her at all. Was she an angel?

Jenny says:

Angels can appear in all sorts of guises. They are pure energy, and as such they can appear in whatever shape or form they choose. They will normally select an appearance that will resonate with us and our situation. The gypsy woman in Jasmine's story was obviously something a child would relate to, as she certainly looked like someone from a fairy tale. I have had various angels appear, as a column of golden light, a rather gorgeous young man with huge white wings, and an elderly lady. So, don't always expect to see a classic, robed being with wings, as this isn't always the case at all.

CHAPTER 3

SHOWN LOVE
BY AN ANGEL

Love is the overriding emotion and comfort we get from our angel friends. Every single person who's been lucky enough to come face to face with an angel has spoken of the love that is given and received by these glorious beings. If ever I have any doubt nowadays about my path, or whether I'm doing the right thing, I just recall that feeling I had when my angel was near and I know that I'm being guided and led.

Some sixteen years or so ago, just before I had my very first soul angel encounter, I was a very different person. When people ask me if they can get help or whether they're a hopeless case, I tell them my story. I had sunk into a deep depression, for which there was no obvious cause. When I was a child, I knew angels and I was the happiest little girl as a result. But parents and teachers, in their attempts to mold me into a "viable member of society" had pretty much severed my connection to my own soul and therefore my angels. While I still had experiences, such as the one related at the beginning of this book, they were isolated incidents as far as I was concerned, and I felt no daily connection, not like I do now. At the time of my depression I was overweight, felt worthless, could not, or did not want to, work because I had no confidence, and was suffering financial hardships. Yet I had a wonderful husband and son, and there was no real reason for my depression. I know now that it was partly due to past-life trauma, but also because I wasn't on my right path, so everything I tried in order to shake myself out of my depression was simply papering over the cracks. I was a classic hopeless case.

After that first angel encounter, my life changed so dramatically that people find it hard to comprehend. I lost weight, started song writing, even penning some award-winning lyrics, found a new career as a television presenter, which I did daily for two years, became a best-selling author, was offered employment as an international magazine columnist, which I still do today, and traveled long-distance to the US, despite a lifelong phobia about flying. If I can do it, so can you!

The next two stories were sent to me as personal emails, and I love them because they validate the work I do—the work that I've been guided to do.

Holly's story:

Difficult Name

I just wanted to let you know that I got your book, and have almost finished reading it, but felt compelled to let you know about the name I found in it for my angel, whom you'd previously painted for me.

From last fall, and gradually gaining momentum until, I would say, a peak moment in March or April, I've been getting messages from heaven. I've been so grateful for these, and yet for some reason find it hard to reach out and accept that I'm worthy of them. I'll receive a message, and every time the voice will tell me to write it down, but for some reason, I never do. I always say, "Thank you! Thank you!" and then later I always wish I'd written it down, just as a way of reassuring myself that it was real.

A few months ago, I received a message about one of your books. I was told that in it you were going to give me the name of my angel, which was difficult to say—Hehewuti. I pictured a Native American woman. I told myself, okay, if the book has that really difficult name in it, I'll know this is real. Needless to say, that is exactly what happened! What's more, reading your book, and all of the stories that sound so similar to things I've experienced, has made me feel a lot more open to what's been happening to me lately. My three-year-old daughter, I can tell, is already very alert and open to the spiritual world (and loves to talk to me about angels)! I realize now that I have to write all of this down, so that even if it's not for me, maybe one day she will be able to

read about the things that the angels have communicated to me, and can communicate to her as well.

Receiving your book is just one of many things that have happened to me this past year. All of them have helped me realize that I need to stay more vigilant, strong, and open to keep receiving these messages, and eventually to help others, although I am still trying to figure that one out!

Angel art

It's extremely gratifying when you receive validation of your work. For me, this is especially true of angel portraits. Some while ago I was told by the angels that I must not accept any payment for that particular part of my work, which I accept. I know that "light-workers," of which I am one, must be very careful not to allow financial reward to figure highly in what they do. And anyway, it is much more satisfying to hear from people that my pictures are helping them in many different and unexpected ways.

I never used to have a talent for portraits at all but now this is my favorite method of connecting people with their angels, and I use it every day. If you'd like to try this and have no natural artistic talent, don't worry, because neither did I when I started out.

✱ Try it onscreen, using a software program, such as Adobe Elements, and just start "drawing" in colors that appeal to you.

✱ When you've filled in a page of colors, use a "smudge" tool to draw through them in quite random ways.

✱ After a while, you'll start to see angel shapes in your abstract pictures. This was what happened with me. First; a few other people started saying that they could see angels in the pictures, and as I continued producing them, gradually the angels became plain for all to see. So keep going and, with a little angel influence, you'll progress, like I did, to creating actual angel art.

Avril's story:

Belief Rekindled

Quite some time ago, I bought your book *Everyday Angels* on a whim and left it in the car, where my daughter Sophie found it. She brought it into the house, put it under the coffee table, and there it stayed for several months.

During the Easter break, my friend Nanette brought her children Toby and Lucie to see us, and after they'd left we found a paper butterfly that Lucie had made, stuck to the windowsill with glue. Kevin, my

partner, finally managed to lift it off in one piece, and balanced it on the mantelpiece, which is not really the place to display a child's art, but it's been there so long, no one really notices it any more.

Several years ago, I read Barbel Mohrs' *Cosmic Ordering for Beginners*, and that was the start of many amazing things. I believed all of them. One of the things she said was that if you think of something and believe it, it will happen, although not always as you assume it will. Sadly, as you know, Barbel died last year. So many bad things had happened that I'd lost faith, and when I found out she'd gone, I suppose I felt that all the things I had believed in had died with her. I researched into death perhaps being an illusion, but could not find anything that had that magic to make me believe again.

One day, I was tidying up in the lounge and remembered what Sophie had said about the photo on the front of one of the books looking like her friend Cally. I picked it up to have a look, and idly began flicking through the pages. I soon became quite engrossed. It was *Everyday Angels*. One story in it was about a young woman who had become close to her granddad. At her wedding, the day after he died, a large blue butterfly appeared. This would have been unusual anyway because they didn't have that many blue butterflies where she lived, but it was also in the middle of a cold November. It stayed with them all through the wedding and then disappeared into thin air. Everyone saw it happen. Now when the woman thinks of her granddad or feels sad or needs help, a blue butterfly turns up, sometimes real, sometimes as an ornament in a store and in many other ways, but it's always there. I burst into tears when I read this because it was what Barbel had said in her book. I thought maybe it was true after all that there is an afterlife, and if it was true, the angels would give me a sign in the next day or two. If they didn't, I'd know it wasn't true.

I opened my eyes and found myself staring straight at Lucie's butterfly! No head movement was required. I did absolutely nothing but open my eyes and there it was, as it had been for weeks, going unnoticed, but now looking wildly out of place as it had originally done, standing out starkly against the background. I opened your book and read the following words: "In this case the butterfly was certainly symbolizing that death is actually just a transition between this state of being and the next one, which will of course be infinitely more beautiful." I knew then that it was true and that there is life after death, and that angels do exist and do listen.

Jenny says:

It's interesting how Avril was seemingly guided to forget about my book until such times as she was ready to accept the message it brought to her. If she'd read it when she bought it, she would most likely have missed the lovely angel connection she received later on. She ended up reading it exactly when she was meant to. We get these little nudges almost every day during our lives, but sometimes the stubbornness of our human nature makes us deliberately ignore the little voice that is trying to get things in the right order for us. Luckily, Avril did listen and in consequence she received a message that will impact on the rest of her life.

Norman's story:

A Long Journey

I used to commute to London on the train, catching the same early-morning train from my local station. Three or four times a year, this train was canceled and when the next train arrived, there was standing room only. On each occasion, I found myself standing next to a middle-aged, nondescript man. We would exchange looks of exasperation, but no words were ever spoken.

One evening in October 1970, I decided that I would not rush for my usual train home, but take it easy and catch the next one, which was due to leave at about 5.50 p.m. I arrived early and found the train was of a type that had small individual cars, each with seating for twelve people. I settled myself in an empty car with the evening paper, and since this time of day was still the rush-hour, I was very surprised that no one else joined me. Just before the train departed, the door opened and in stepped the middle-aged, nondescript man that I had stood next to on so many train journeys. We nodded at each other politely, and I carried on reading.

"You're a Cancerian, aren't you?" he asked. Although I had some interest in horoscopes, I simply gave him an uninterested, cynical look. "Ah, a nonbeliever," he then said, and proceeded to tell me something about myself that was very personal and close to me, which no one else knew. Now he had my attention!

He started talking about our lives as if he were outside, looking in. I was at the very beginning of my spiritual journey and struggled to understand what was being said. After a while, he leaned his head to one side and looked at me pensively, probably thinking, "How can I get through to him?" After a few seconds, he asked me, "Which record is number one in the music charts?" Well, this both surprised and confused me. He didn't look like somebody who would know anything about current music, and it was an unexpected change of subject.

After a few seconds' thought, I replied, " 'Woodstock' by Matthews Southern Comfort."

"That's right," he said, "and what's the chorus line?"

Again, I was surprised and had to think for a few seconds before answering, "We are stardust, we are golden, and we've got to get ourselves back to the garden."

"That's right," he said. "That's all you need to know." Just before my station, he leaned forward, smiled, and said, "Life is a long, long journey... but you're almost there."

My normal twenty-minute walk home took nearly an hour that day, and it was as if I was in a trance. My mind kept going over and over what he had said. I never saw the man again. The whole episode is as fresh today as it was forty years ago and I think about it regularly.

Jenny says: Right place, right time. Norman was obviously teetering on the brink of revelation in his spiritual journey, and this kindly, caring stranger was in exactly the right place at exactly the right time to tip him over into his real life. It can be no coincidence that Norman was directed to alter his journey that day, and the conversation couldn't have comfortably taken place if the train car had other people in it, so the isolation was perfect, too. Like Avril, Norman allowed himself to be led to the right moment. Remember this story, and if someone starts up a conversation as interesting as this one, give it a chance, because you, too, might be entertaining an angel who loves you, and if you're not aware and open, you might miss the whole thing!

CHAPTER 4

HELPED IN MY GRIEF BY AN ANGEL

Grief caused by the loss of a loved one is one of the most difficult states we ever have to cope with. Even if you believe, as I do, that the soul never dies and can, in fact, reincarnate into a new body, you still have to accept the fact that the physical person you called mom or dad, or who was your child or best friend, is not going to be there in the physical plane any more. If that person has been taken out of pain, we have to try to be glad for them, but still, we miss their presence. Angels have been known to help in these circumstances, sometimes with appearances that bring comfort, sometimes by bringing through a message from the person who has passed over, and sometimes by performing what seem like miracles in the time leading up to their departing the Earth.

Losing a child has to be the most heart-wrenching bereavement to endure, and it would take a huge experience that was totally convincing to ease such pain. Babies have special angels, and I have been sent many accounts over the years that have proved this to me. This seems to be particularly relevant when very young, or even unborn, children pass away.

Jen's story:

Touch of an Angel's Wings

I was grief-stricken when my mom died, aged seventy-four. It was no age really, and besides her terminal illness, she'd been quite good for her age so I wasn't ready (are you ever?) for her to leave me. For the next four years I felt hellish. I had this awful thought that it was all pointless and that we were all just waiting to die. I pretty much was useless for my family, and just sat and cried a lot. I was sitting at home one day, still in my bathrobe, and just eating and crying alternately, thinking I really should pull myself together for our son's sake if nothing else, but what was the point? Then I felt a tingling as something feathery gently brushed across my shoulders. I got goose-bumps all over. I realized that a scent of freesias, my mom's

favorite flower, was wafting over me. My mood lifted, and that was when I heard her voice. She said, "What you have to do now is think about what I want for you. I want the same for you as you'd want for your son if you had died. What I want is for you to be strong and independent. Isn't that what you want for your own child? We do all die, but that isn't the end, so pick yourself up and start being a parent!" Then something touched me again and my mom was gone. I believe now that once we're ready, an angel can bring a loved one through to us. I believe the touch I felt was that of an angel's wings.

Jenny says: It's amazing how loved ones who have passed over can suddenly speak such words of wisdom to us, words that they might have struggled to find while alive. Of course, once they pass over they are given divine knowledge. Angels work very hard to make this kind of communication happen. If a soul tried to achieve it alone, it would be very difficult. Angels have to be present to lift the veil and allow the words or the touch or the scent or the vision to come through to us.

Carmen's story:

Light Fantastic

My mother, whom I adored, died in the UK while I was living here in Australia. My family had stopped me from going to be with her while she passed over. My mother was my life, my strength, my heart-beat. The day of her funeral I went to the big Catholic cathedral in Perth city. Although I was not, nor am I, religious, I did often go to talk to St Theresa in bad times. Why? Who knows? Had to have someone—with possible connections to the big guy—to talk to, I guess.

On this occasion, I was so distraught that I asked God to take me to be with my mom. I could not live without her. I was sitting there, begging St Theresa to help me. I felt I couldn't go on, but I had two children to think about. I was confused, wanting to die to be with my mom, but also to live for my children. I wept like my heart would break. When I looked up at St Theresa, a bright blue light shone like a halo but at her feet. I blinked, and it was still there but had moved up her body. I shut my eyes and turned my head away, but as soon as I looked back, it started to rise again. I did this several times and each time I opened my eyes the light moved. So I watched and my mind seemed to be taken over. My brain went numb. The whole of St Theresa's head, neck, and shoulders were bathed in this brilliant bright blue light. I was mesmerized, my mind gone. I could not feel anything.

Jenny says: Angels often use light anomalies to communicate with us nowadays. Some of these light effects can even be caught on camera. If Carmen had had one with her that day, she might have been able to capture the angelic blue light, which could then have brought her permanent comfort.

I faintly remember leaving the cathedral and knew no more until I got home. How I got there, I don't know. I must have gone to bed, because I woke there some time later, drained, but that crushing desire to die, that all encompassing grief, had lifted. I knew I would go on living. Was that an angel or angels? I still weep for my mom nearly twenty years later, but when I get to that breaking point, whatever/whoever seems to take me over and numb my mind, and I know I can go on again.

Color-coded photo messages

If you feel you could communicate with your angels in this way, try the following.

✻ First of all, tell your angels what you intend to do. Say something like, "May I have a red orb for no and a blue one for yes?"

✻ Make a list of colors and their significance to you. More answers can be provided by misty and colored shapes.

✻ Once you've established your code, take photos whenever the fancy strikes you of whatever your intuition pulls you toward. It's always a good idea to keep an eye on pets and babies, because they often see spirits and energy that we don't.

✻ See what you capture. Most importantly, when you do capture something and the orb or mist appears to correspond to your question, don't let logic click in and make you doubt. You asked and you were answered. It's as simple as that.

Melody's story:

A Room of Her Own

Most kids I knew didn't take too much notice of their grandparents, but my nan was different. My parents were killed in a car crash when I was a baby and Nan brought me up, so she was more like a mom. Of course, this meant she was quite old, and by the time I had a husband and baby of my own, I knew she wouldn't be around much longer. We moved her into our guest room when she got ill and it was awful watching her go downhill. Even so, when I got the call it seemed so sudden, and I never had a chance to say goodbye. I was out of town, and I was devastated. She'd always been there, and now she wasn't. My son Joseph, who was five years old, had loved her, too, and I know he missed her. I prayed that I'd get some sign but I never did.

One day when I collected Joseph from school, he said something very odd. He said he had to wait for his friend in the backyard. This was odd because he'd recently had his sixth birthday and usually couldn't wait to get to his room to play with his new game. Also, it was a bit chilly, plus there's no way into our backyard from the road, so I didn't see how any friend could meet him there. He said his friend's name was Zach, and I didn't know any such kid in his class. I said he could wait there, because he really wanted to, but I kept an eye on him from the kitchen window. He sat on the bench at the bottom of the garden and after a while he suddenly got up, smiling, as if he was pleased to see someone. But there was no one there. Then he started talking. I could see his lips moving, but couldn't hear what he was saying. Suddenly, he did a little skip and clapped his hands, and turned to look at me, a big smile on his face. He waved, I waved back, and he came running up the path. He told me that his friend Zach had come, and he'd brought a message from Nan. The message was that I really should clear her things out of the house because the new baby would need a room of her own soon. I was totally amazed, because what I'd never got the chance to tell Nan, and what Joseph didn't know, was that I was finally pregnant with a much longed for sibling for Joseph. Not only that, just that day the scan had revealed that I was carrying a baby girl.

Jenny says:

This experience will touch the lives of several people — Joseph, because hopefully his mother will keep reminding him about it so he doesn't forget the angel called Zach who came to visit and was his friend; Melody herself, and her husband; and the little girl, yet to be born. I have a feeling that the last part of this puzzle might be that the little girl will be born with memories of a much-loved nan because, who knows, she might actually have been that nan.

Suzanne's story:

Face in the Clouds

My father passed away and when we were scattering his ashes over Lake Tahoe, I looked up and I could see several pastel-colored angels looking down on us. I could see my father's face among them and it gave me great comfort knowing that he was with the angels, and that I saw it!

Jenny says: It's very easy to dismiss this kind of thing as wishful thinking, and we can all only go by our own personal experiences. However, there's nothing to lose and everything to gain by keeping an open heart. If you've lost someone dear to you and you're desperately asking for a sign from them, do keep an open mind. It's not coincidence, in my mind, that a cloud closely resembling a loved one's face should be brought into being just as the grieving person is asking for a connection. Likewise, rainbows that appear unexpectedly, just as someone is praying for help, are a sign that help is there in the form of an angel.

Natural messengers

I once did a telephone reading for Jackiey Budden, the mother of TV celebrity Jade Goody who died of cancer in 2009. Just as I felt Jade's spirit arrive in the room with her mother, Jackiey cried out that the curtains in the airless room had lifted toward the ceiling as if blown there, so angels will make use of wind. During that same reading, I described a butterfly to Jackiey. It was a lemon-colored insect with creamy colored tips to its wings. Jackiey told me that this same butterfly had been following her around for days.

Someone else wrote to me and told me that a bird had come down the chimney a few days after her father had died. It had shown no fear of the family and had tracked sooty footprints all over the carpet until it jumped onto her father's chair, and just perched there. Needless to say, the family were astounded and started talking about what it could mean. It was the letter-writer who said she thought it was a messenger from her dad. The bird sat there quietly, appearing to watch the television, until it was almost dark, and then calmly jumped onto the window ledge and tapped the glass as if asking to be let out.

Joan's story:

Baby Angel

I knew there was something wrong because my baby hadn't moved inside me for several days, but I didn't want to accept it. I was on my way to the hospital to have a scan, simply to confirm what I already knew, and I was broken by it. I could barely see to drive for the tears that were streaming down my cheeks. I was so upset I hadn't even told my husband or my mother, and I still haven't told them this story. Anyway, I was driving myself because I couldn't find the words to tell anyone but the doctors. I hadn't been pregnant very long and didn't even know if I was carrying a girl or a boy. I was nearly there, and I knew that once the scan was done, they would remove my child, and I was still clinging to the baby's presence, so I pulled over to collect my wits.

As soon as I'd switched off the engine, my eyes closed and I found it impossible to open them. I don't know if I was awake or asleep, but I could still hear the traffic. Finally, my eyes opened, and where the windscreen should have been there was a bright, blinding light. It filled with white fluffy clouds and out of them emerged the most beautiful face I have ever seen. I could not say if it was a man or a woman. The face smiled and glowing arms reached down to me. As they pulled back, I could see a tiny glowing ball in the hands. "He will be safe now. He will return when the time is right," the being said, and withdrew into the clouds, taking what I knew to be my baby's soul with it. I came around and drove on to the hospital. I went through the scan and what followed with a heart that, while not mended, wasn't still shattered into a million pieces.

Eternally in spirit

Angels often communicate with me in the middle of the night, and one of the most poignant things that I have learned, which is relevant to this chapter, is that none of us is ever alone in the spirit world. We can't be because everyone we ever knew and loved is always there, too. This might not make sense until I explain the rest of the information. All of us, every single one—man, woman, child, or even unborn baby—we always have the greatest of ourselves in spirit. This part remains and never leaves. The part of us that comes to inhabit our earthly bodies is a very small part of our souls, a mere spark. The rest of us, our greatest and most wonderful part, is eternally in spirit, waiting to greet souls that have passed over. So no mother need ever worry that her child is lost and alone and missing her in heaven, because she is there, too. You are never separated from a loved one, not even for a second; it's just that our mortal bodies and minds on Earth can't see or hear them, but in reality we're always with them.

Six months later I was pregnant again, and I didn't need a scan this time to tell me I was carrying a little boy, because the night he was conceived I had another dream. On this occasion the angel, for that was surely what it was, returned the little orb to my body. Our son was born, healthy and happy, and from that moment I didn't mourn for the baby who had died any more, because I knew he had come back, this time to stay.

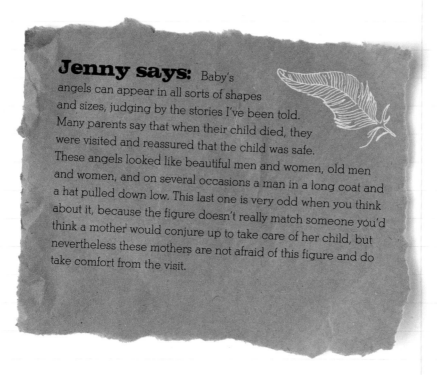

Jenny says: Baby's angels can appear in all sorts of shapes and sizes, judging by the stories I've been told. Many parents say that when their child died, they were visited and reassured that the child was safe. These angels looked like beautiful men and women, old men and women, and on several occasions a man in a long coat and a hat pulled down low. This last one is very odd when you think about it, because the figure doesn't really match someone you'd think a mother would conjure up to take care of her child, but nevertheless these mothers are not afraid of this figure and do take comfort from the visit.

Animal messengers

Angels can even bring through a message from beloved pets that have passed away. My big, black Labrador cross, Ace, was like a child or a soul mate to me, and after she died I was distraught and grief-stricken. I had her cremated and buried her ashes beneath an especially selected rose tree, called Shine On, which I thought was appropriate. One day I was being filmed by a television crew from an Australian TV show, and talking about my angel experiences. I was thinking how wonderful it would be if something actually happened on camera. We were drawn to talk while standing around Ace's rose tree, talking about Ace, and with me voicing my desire to have a message from her, when one, then two, then all of us, including the producer, suddenly started to comment on the heat that seemed to be coming from the flame-colored roses on the tree. The heat from the whole tree grew more and more intense as if we were actually standing in front of a fire. We all looked at each other in astonishment, and afterwards we said how our faces had been glowing with light from the invisible flames. I know this was a message that my angel brought through from my dear Ace, to comfort me. She couldn't have said any clearer, "don't worry, Mom, I do shine on."

There's no reason to exclude our pets from the world of angels. In many ways they find a connection to angels easier than we humans do. This is because they are more natural creatures and have their intuitions and instincts intact, whereas we have lost them to a large extent. Also animals have a more balanced energy, which comes from their ability to look neither forward nor back, but instead to live in the moment, and this kind of "smooth" energy is the easiest kind for angels to work within.

CHAPTER 5

WARNED BY AN ANGEL

Sometimes our lives seem to run on rails, and everything that's supposed to happen does happen, but because we are all human, things do go wrong. This is obvious and I really don't subscribe to the theory that everything that happens is meant to happen, because we do have free will. It would be impossible, if you think about it, for every single person always to do and say exactly what they're meant to—a single word can literally change the course of someone's history. Not only that, how would any being, even one as powerful as God, keep our lives in order, when they are like some incredibly complicated 3D cosmic jigsaw puzzles and we are able at any time to choose to go against our ordained direction?

We're all affected by what everyone else does, and sometimes what someone else does, or what happens to them, can knock us off our paths. I do believe that we all have a path that we are meant to tread, but I also believe things can go off track. This is where angels will step in to help get us back on track. We may be warned in some way to do something different from what we planned, with amazing consequences. We may be warned about something that is happening, or about to happen, to a loved one, and that very warning, and the train of thought it creates, can be the catalyst that gets us back to where we were meant to be. Sometimes we gain an inner core of strength from the angel encounter, which enables us to withstand circumstances that might otherwise have crushed us.

Jada's story:

Looking Out for a Friend

I'm a professional singer/songwriter and I live in the California gold country. Here's my story. I was hired as a "spokesmodel" for the Indy Car 500 event, which meant that, together with an Indy car representative, Troy, I had to do "meet and greets" in the local bars in Silicon Valley to help promote the Indy Car 500 races. Troy spent pretty much all year traveling around the country and setting up these Indy 500 promotional events. Long story short, we had some chemistry and casually dated during the two weeks we were working together.

After he left Silicon Valley, his next stop was Los Angeles for two weeks. Soon after Troy left for LA, I got a horrible feeling that he was in mortal danger. My stomach actually tightened up and I got very scared for him. I called his cell phone many times but was unable to reach him. So I prayed for God to send an angel to protect him. Finally, a week later, Troy returned my phone calls and said that he was in hospital, where he'd been for a week. He said that he was at one of his

Indy 500 events at a bar in LA, when a group of Samoan guys started hassling him. Troy told me that they would not leave him alone, and one of them started beating him up. He was so big that no one came to help Troy. It went on for about five minutes and then the men moved on, leaving Troy lying on the floor of the bar. Troy told me that as he was lying there he knew that he was going to die, but then he suddenly got a feeling that someone was watching over him. This gives me chills just writing about it. I already knew that Troy was not a religious person from spending time with him, but he said that he sure felt like something saved his life that day.

Jenny says: I think most people who believe in angels, believe that they can call on them in times of danger. Jada's story shows that maybe you can call on them to help others, too. I'm not so sure about that, though. I really feel that normally each person can only ask their own angel for help. Perhaps in this case Jada was actually in touch with Troy, rather than her angel, and because of that Troy was inspired subconsciously to ask his own angel for help.

Virtual star crystal

What should you do if you want angelic help for someone else? By all means ask your angels to help if they can, but I've come across another way to do this that seems to work very well. One night when I was connected to my angel, I was handed a virtual angel star crystal. This is something I see in my mind's eye, which is different for each person I'm trying to send help to. I either hand it to the person, if he/she is open to the suggestion, or if not, I visualize inserting it into his/her aura. I believe everyone has the ability to do this. It's a sort of "fast track" switch for another person's angel. I think it temporarily raises that person's vibration to a point where his/her angel can connect and help, often without the person being aware of what's happening.

If you know someone who doesn't seem to be able to make a connection with his/her angels, try "seeing" one of these imaginary crystals in your mind's eye and offer it to your friend. All I can say is that I have seen these wonderful things work on many occasions. For instance, one lady I knew was terrified that she was losing her daughter to a bad crowd. The girl had changed character and become abusive and unloving toward her family. Within a few days, the situation had completely changed and the mother felt she had her daughter back from the brink.

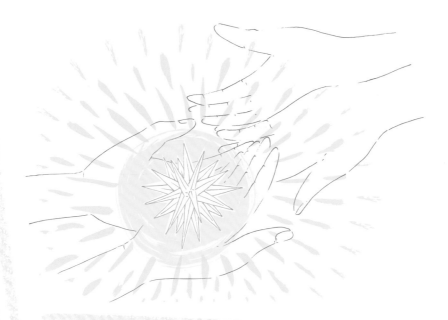

Mandy's story:

Bidding Farewell

My best friend and I were having a slumber party in my parents' living room. During the night I awoke suddenly and sat up. The room was very bright and I saw a figure in the light. It was a young woman— I didn't recognize her face—and she was smiling at me. Soon the light went away and the room went dark again. I remember looking over at my friend and seeing that she was still sound asleep. In the morning, I contemplated whether my parents would believe me if I told them what I'd seen or if they'd dismiss it. But before I could say anything about it, my dad pulled me aside to tell me the sad news that my beloved great-grandmother had died during the night. I like to think that the light I saw that night was a younger version of her smiling down at me, as if to say goodbye.

Jenny says:

What Mandy saw may indeed have been the spirit of her great-grandmother, brought through by an angel and lit with angel-light. I believe that when we pass over, we remain in appearance at the age we most enjoyed during our lives, which would explain why Mandy's great-grandmother looked young.

Dianne's story:

A Father's Care

My daughter Jenny was about fifteen when she appeared in the middle of our room late one night. "He's back, Mom," she said. Since she was eight, Jenny had occasionally been seeing a mysterious light in her bedroom, and two years ago she had seen an image of a man emerge from it. I have to admit this time I was a little shaken and sent my

husband Mark to check things out for a change. He stomped into Jenny's room, boomed out a few expletives to the supposed ghost, and said to Jenny, "That oughta do it!" But when he came back, he told me, "I felt something. It's freezing in one corner of her room." That was odd, because it was summertime in Queensland, Australia.

The next morning Jenny described what she had seen in detail. A soldier with a pointy cap had appeared from a bright light, and stood at the foot of her bed, but she had not felt threatened by him. All I could think of was that this was some kind of warning. On the off chance, I showed Jenny a photograph of my husband's late father, Robert, in Vietnam in an army uniform but the figure wasn't him.

Messaging devices

Angels are not averse to using outside agencies to get a message to us—answerphones, dictaphones, or even old-fashioned tape recorders. If this method of communication appeals to you, here's what to do.

✳ Set up your chosen device in a quiet place where it's unlikely that there'll be any disturbances or vibrations that might make extraneous sounds on the machine. Start the machine running.

✳ Close your eyes and imagine your angel standing right behind you.

✳ Speaking in a clear voice, ask your angel to speak to you, and then allow time for an answer to be recorded on the machine.

✳ Angels will sometimes come through as the sound of tinkling bells, breezes, whistles, or a singing bowl. If you're really lucky, you may get an actual voice.

I never knew my father, Jan. He passed away when I was a year old. A large black-and-white photograph of him in a Polish Second World War army uniform, wearing a square peaked cap, used to hang in the dining room when I was growing up. My brother had the photograph now, and he lived in Sydney. I got in touch and asked him to send me a copy, but I never mentioned it to Jenny. The photograph arrived one afternoon when Jenny was at the computer. I walked into the study and placed the photograph on the keyboard, without saying anything. Instantaneously, she began to cry. "That's him, Mom! That's him!" From that day, he never returned to her.

Jenny says: In a case like this, it's good to find a photograph of the person you think may be visiting, when they were young, if you can, and compare the recent experience with what they looked like then. This idea came in very useful to Dianne.

A short while later, I was diagnosed with a rare neurological disorder, myasthenia gravis. It's now been four years since the diagnosis, and although there have been some serious moments, I'm managing the disease. Jenny's visions affirmed my belief that my father was my guardian angel and I take comfort in believing he's still around. Jenny has never mentioned her visions to anyone outside our family.

CHAPTER 6

HELPED BY AN ANGEL

Everyday signs of angels include unexpected white feathers; flowers, especially roses, appearing where there were none before; a certain scent that fills the air; even a vision of a spectral figure or an unearthly light. Some people who work with their angels all the time receive signs that they've come to accept and depend upon, such as a shiver down the spine, just like you'd get if someone tickled you with a feather; a feeling of cobwebs across the face; or perhaps a gentle hand on the brow. Others hear music from no obvious source. This happened to me once in the middle of the night. We live in a rural area, our neighbors were away, and it was like no music I'd ever heard before. The signs are myriad, and once you start asking your angel questions and expecting to receive answers, you'll soon develop your own signals of a connection being made.

Chelsey's story:

Angel of Calm

This is a little experience I had about five years ago when I was due to take my driving test. I took a relaxing bath that morning and asked my angel and my grandfather, who had passed to spirit, to give me the strength and confidence to pass the test. I also asked for a sign that they'd heard me. Before leaving for the test center, I pushed a picture of my granddad into my back pocket. I was sitting in my instructor's

car, going through everything I had to remember. The sun was shining and we had the windows down, literally two inches. All of a sudden, a white feather floated through that small gap and landed by the gearshift. I was so excited, and kept saying to my instructor, "Is that a feather? Is that a feather?" I must have sounded like a mad woman! He couldn't understand what all the fuss was about, so I explained what I'd done, although I'm not sure she believed in it. I put the feather in my pocket with the picture of my granddad, and set off on my test. I made a couple of silly mistakes, but the thought of the feather helped me to stay calm and I rectified them straightaway. When we got back to the test center, I was convinced I must have failed, but amazingly I had passed! The man who tested me said that even though I'd made the mistakes, he still passed me because I'd stayed calm and tried again. I was delighted, and I believe my granddad and my angel were right there with me, keeping me calm.

Jenny says: Chelsey gives a perfect example of how receiving a small sign can help. The fact that she acknowledged it changed the whole dynamic of her situation, and the consequent change in her energy also changed the way she was viewed by the examiner. Although Chelsey was still nervous about failing her test, the angel sign gave her enough confidence to keep her composure, which impressed her examiner enough for him to allow her to pass. If you're facing a test or an examination of any kind, whether it be academic, an interview, or even a medical check-up, my advice is to ask your angels for help. Whatever the outcome is going to be, having an angel by your side will enable you to be calm, to impress others with your confidence, and to have the strength to see the test through.

Katherine's story:

Angel of Comfort

Back when I was fourteen, I was going through a difficult time because a special person in my life was moving away. I was very upset and behaved spitefully toward him. One night I went to bed, crying, so angry and also sad for the way things were happening. Later, I woke up choking, and as I tried to catch my breath, I saw a lady with long dark hair standing beside my bed. She shone with such brightness and was so

peaceful. I was still choking, trying to comprehend who she was, yet not feeling at all worried that someone was in my room. I could see the tips of her wings behind her back and felt the coolness of refreshing essence as she reached out to touch my head. She stroked my hair and spoke to me in a soothing voice. "Everything will be okay, go back to sleep." I had stopped choking, and asked her who she was, what was happening. She smiled and lightly stroked my eyelids to close them, whispering, "Go to sleep now, Katherine, everything will be okay." It was like I was under a spell, trying to remain awake because I wanted to talk to her. I saw her beauty and felt such love, and I was so at peace. I fell asleep.

A son's connection

Of course, tragically, not all children can be saved. In one case I know about, a child was killed in a road accident. His mother told me she had been vacuuming, not worrying about her two sons, who were out on their bikes, and who were always very careful. Then she suddenly heard her younger son calling out her name above the sound of the vacuum. She switched it off immediately and listened, but there was nothing, and so she continued vacuuming, thinking she'd imagined it, or mistaken a dog's bark for the voice. She wrote to me, devastated because if she had left the house when she heard the voice, she might just have made it to her son before he passed away. Instead, she was notified of his death by a police officer half an hour later. Her guilt was destroying her life, and also preventing her from being there for her other son, who had survived the accident.

I'm not a medium but as soon as I asked, my angels brought the boy through to me where I sat in front of my computer, reading the mother's sad email. Thanks to my angels, I was able to hear enough from the boy to convince his mother totally that he still existed, that he didn't blame her, and one day they would be together again. I'm pleased to say that she went on to cope with her grief and make a good life for her other son.

In the morning, I asked my momma if she had been in my room the night before. Even though I remembered the angel, a part of me thought maybe I had just dreamed it and it was really my mother. She said that she had been in the living room when she heard me choking, and so had hurried to check on me. She heard me speaking to someone, but I was sleeping peacefully when she came in. I just knew that I had gotten to see my guardian angel, and I felt so thankful for that moment. It was such a gift. Over the years, I've often wondered if I'd ever see her again, yet in my heart, I still feel her stroking my hair at times when I can't sleep and I curl up and ask her to help me relax.

Jenny says:

Mothers have an inbuilt connection to angels where their children are concerned, and I have read many stories in which a mother received a warning that her children were in danger and has been able to act to save them. Moms are constantly tuned in to their intuition when it comes to their children, and so perhaps they are more able to receive these kinds of messages.

Mary's story:

Always a Reason

In the late 1980s, my husband, daughter, son, and I were at the dinner table one evening in late April, and I was telling my husband that I had noticed the umbrella from our outdoor table was missing. There had been a storm the night before, and I thought it must have blown out of its socket, but I couldn't find it. At this, my daughter, who was about six at the time, said, "Dear God, please bring back our umbrella!" Literally, two minutes later, the doorbell rang, and an Asian man stood at the door, holding our umbrella. He told us that he had found it in his yard, three houses down. I took the umbrella and closed the door. Five seconds later I realized I hadn't thanked him, opened the door to do so, and he was not there. He could not have gotten out of sight that quickly. Still, I did not think much of it until later, when I remembered that our only Asian neighbors lived at the top of the hill. Our umbrella could not possibly have blown that far. Also, how could he have known that it was our umbrella? Our deck was hidden from the street by the walls of our house on the west and in front, and by bushes on the eastern and southern sides. We were never able to use the umbrella again, due to some damage, so I could not figure out why it was actually returned to us like that, except for the fact that my daughter had prayed. I have to believe that an angel came to return our umbrella and, more importantly, to teach a little girl to keep praying because God listens to and answers our prayers.

One evening in 2008, when I left work at around 8.30, it was snowing heavily and the wind had picked up. Fortunately, traffic was light, and I was fine going slowly until I turned off the highway and onto the twisting roads that led to my house. I crept along, trying to keep to the road through the swirling snow, but took a wrong turn. I started to back up but had to stop. I couldn't see anything. Now I was scared, and prayed to get home safely. I thought about sitting it out, but that could be hours and it was really cold outside. Besides, I have hypoglycemia (low blood sugar) and I hadn't eaten dinner yet, so sitting for hours would have made me too dizzy to drive. I picked up my cell phone to call my husband, and as I looked in my rearview mirror I saw an SUV with his flashers on coming toward me. I instantly decided to follow that car, hoping he was going my way, and waited about ten seconds for him and another car to pass me. The other car went straight, but the SUV turned my way. I followed him all the way to my street, where he turned right and I turned left. As I straightened the car, I quickly looked in my rearview mirror to see the SUV, but there was nothing there. I'm certain I'd have seen him, because I had drawn up almost next to him as we turned, and he couldn't have disappeared so quickly into the snow with the flashers going. I surely would have seen him. After all, I was still able to see him before, even with another car between us, and the snow was a bit lighter now. My conclusion is that God answered my desperate prayers to get home safely by sending this guiding angel. I am grateful for this, but to this day, I will not drive at night in blowing snow.

Jenny says: I particularly loved the story about the umbrella, because it was so unusual and seemingly so unimportant. Mary's daughter will never forget how her prayers were answered and, who knows, in her adult life this might become a vital part of her makeup. If it allows her to follow her rightful path, that may be something to do with why it happened. Another reason may be to do with preparation. Mary didn't really understand at the time why she got the first sign, since the umbrella was useless anyway, but perhaps it happened in order to prepare her to accept angel help the second time it came. If she hadn't, she might well have died that night.

Jo's story:

Helpful Angels

When I do reiki, I always ask the angels to help me. I feel them there, adding their healing energy and light. One evening I was giving healing to a friend, and I could feel three angels helping. After his treatment, he asked, "Who else was here?" He'd had his eyes closed. "No one," I answered. "There were at least three other people here," he said. "I felt their hands on me, and when I opened my eyes I saw their feet. I thought it was you, but you were at the other end of the therapy bed."

My parents had just celebrated their pearl wedding anniversary, and my dad had given my mom a beautiful (and very expensive!) pair of pearl earrings. My mom and I went to Paris for a weekend shortly afterward, and my mom lost one of the earrings. We searched literally everywhere, checking every square inch of our hotel room. In the morning we retraced our steps from the day before. In the end, I suggested to Mom that she ask the angels to help her. At the time, I think she was just humoring me, but she asked. We decided to go out for coffee before catching the Eurostar home, closing the window shutters as we left our room. When we got back and opened the door, we were just in awe. A very bright light from the shutters fell onto the carpet, illuminating the pearl earring! It was just glowing with light! Mom couldn't believe it. I knew that the angels would find the earring, and they made a believer out of Mom, too!

Jenny says: I've often had angels help me find lost items. Once it was our one and only backdoor key in the middle of a field of long grass. This reminds me, too, of some mischievous little beings that I call "elementals." People often realize the existence of these supernatural creatures in their homes after items have mysteriously gone missing only to reappear somewhere unexpected a few days later. Some people would probably call these beings fairies, and I don't know who is right. I have seen them both as fluttering bright lights in the garden, and also as dark specks that rush across the carpet, just on the edge of vision. Whatever they are, as well as being mischievous, they can be very helpful, as in the case of the missing earring.

Practical help

Occasionally, elementals can actually repair electrical items. How or why they do this, I don't know, but they've done it for us more than once. The rear wipers on Tony's car had been going slower and slower until they jammed. At the time we were very short of money and really couldn't afford new blades. Someone had told me that the elementals could be helpful, so I asked them, and the next morning, low and behold, the wipers worked as good as new. We never had another problem with them all the time we had the car. So, if you have something like this happen, just ask, because you never know what the outcome might be.

Liz's story:

Operational Safeguard

My husband John was waiting to go into hospital for a heart bypass operation, and I was pretty uptight, to put it mildly. For months, every night before going to bed, I asked the angels to keep John safe and help him come through the surgery. The first thing that happened was that I received a photo on my phone of an angel poem from an author whose book I had read. I had not been in touch with her, and when I emailed she replied that she had no idea how I received the message because she hadn't sent it. She came back to me a couple of hours later to say it was my mother (who had passed) who had sent the poem, because she knew I was worrying about something and wanted me to know that she was helping things from spirit.

A week or so before John went in for his operation, I was sleeping in the spare room—I had been unable to get to sleep and went next door so as not to disturb him. At some point I woke up and the room just felt odd, and looked sort of misty. I had been facing the wall and turned around so that I was facing the window, and there, clear as day, silhouetted on the drapes, which were plain purple, was a beautiful

young angel with long red hair. She wore a white robe with a sash around the waist, and was holding what I think was a book. Strangely, I was mesmerized by her feet—bare and porcelain-like, but small and very fine. I sat up watching her for about thirty seconds and then she disappeared. I've always believed in angels and I knew for sure that John would be all right, and he was.

Sheila's story:

A Personal Message

For two years, everything was going wrong for me and mine. My son was so ill that he nearly died. I lost my job after twenty-six years, my husband Steve lost his job, and then we nearly lost our home. I became so depressed that I wanted to die. I felt that I'd lost everything I'd worked for.

Then about two months ago, I read your book, *Everyday Angels*, and turned to the angels for help. I've always believed in angels but never knew how to ask for their help before. I first asked them to help me find a way to dig myself out of my financial situation, and within two days my husband found a job. It was incredible to know that there really was help out there for us.

Steve and I went on vacation to Gran Canaria, and on the flight out he was sitting on the opposite side of the aisle from me. I'm nervous

about flying, so I asked the angels to give me a smooth flight, and it was great. I was so calm, it was unbelievable. On vacation, I felt more relaxed than I had done in years, and all because when I needed help, it was given. Two names for my angels came into my mind, Jack and Nathan, and when we were standing in line to check-in for our flight home, I asked Jack and Nathan if they could make sure I got a seat next to Steve this time. We got two seats together. I'm so amazed how wonderful the angels are, and even Steve is starting to think so, too.

I felt so positive that I decided to take a couple of courses, and passed them with the help of my wonderful angels. I'm also taking a victim support course, because the angels have shown me which path to follow. I lost my way somewhere along the line and now I'm starting to see a light at the end of the tunnel. I could go on and on, and I want to thank you and my angels for the guidance you've given me. I had to write to you, and maybe my tale will help others, too.

Monica's story:

Taxi!

In 1996 I was doing a tarot workshop in London, and had to get back to Sweden the next day to pick up my son from nursery school. Check-in at Stansted Airport was 5.30 a.m. latest, so I booked a taxi for 3 a.m. to take me to the train station. I was devastated when it didn't show up. There were no taxis about on the roadds at that time, but suddenly a black cab appeared. The driver, a little old wrinkly man, asked me where I was going, so I told him Liverpool Street Station, and off we went. Once we got there, he refused payment. I couldn't understand why. I was distressed and he knew that, but he still had a living to earn. It got stranger. Once I was out of the cab, I turned to wave by way of a thank-you, but it was nowhere to be seen. I'm convinced that a lovely angel came to my rescue in this unexpected guise.

Carmen's story:

Healing Prints

I meant to tell you. I was so moved by your angel portraits on Facebook that I printed some of them. My daughter Kim was looking at them at a time when her shoulder was very hot and painful, and we were worried that an infection had set in. She put the pictures on the arm of the chair while we were talking, resting her arm on them, and she suddenly said, "Mom, there's a weird feeling going up my arm!" She took her arm off the pictures and it stopped, so she placed her arm back on top of them. Within a few hours her shoulder had cooled down and it did not hurt anywhere near as much. I think these angels may do healing!

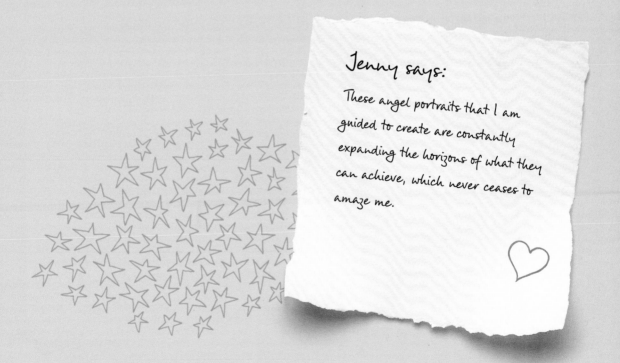

Jenny says:

These angel portraits that I am guided to create are constantly expanding the horizons of what they can achieve, which never ceases to amaze me.

Chapter 7

An angel changed my path

A curve ball from an angel might sound odd, but that's the best description I have for these unexpected signs and messages that make us swerve from what we thought was our path. One of the keys to being happy and fulfilled is constantly to pay attention to these things, and accept when we're being guided, or re-assigned, either to a new and different path or, indeed, back onto a previous one where we should have stayed, but from which we took a diversion.

We all have a path that we're meant to walk, but we spend half our lives trying to figure out what that is. Our own intuition may be screaming at us not to do something, but our stubborn resistance to "being told what to do" means that even when we know in our heart of hearts that we shouldn't do it, we still often go the wrong way. In these cases, we need the help of a hefty nudge from our angels to stop us making a big mistake.

Mickey's story:

Getting Back on Track

"How could it say positive? Why does it say positive? This is NOT a positive thing!" I was standing hunched over the bathroom sink in a friend's apartment in Tempe, Arizona, wearing a swimsuit top and black cut-off shorts with a bright yellow Batman insignia on the back pocket. My friend, looking over my shoulder at the pregnancy testing kit, confirmed, "It's positive," and went back to heating up our toaster waffles. I knew my life was about to change, but I had no idea that it would change so completely, and I really had no idea it would alter every part of the rest of my path. Now, as I look back, this was the one day when every part of my fate, fortune, and viewpoint was shifted for ever. Right there in the toaster waffle bathroom it was starting to unfold.

The idea of becoming an unmarried mother was an awful future to contemplate, and the circumstances surrounding my pregnancy were not too hot, either. This was not the life I was looking for. I'd just moved across the country, and I was in my dream job, involving travel and living in the sunshine. Pregnant and single was not part of my plan. I made the dreaded appointment at the clinic. I remember feeling all day that I should just run and hide. Being committed to my future,

I just ignored the urge to run away and kept going on a route that made me uncomfortable. I wanted to keep on the path I was "supposed" to be on. I lied to myself that no one would ever know—I'd take the weekend off and not tell a soul what was really going on. I could "fix" this mis-step.

At the clinic, I was ushered into room three and got undressed. The room was lined with dark wood paneling and had a green shagpile carpet that must have been there since 1975. The room looked like an insurance office that had got lost in time. It even smelled like it. This place was a dump. I sighed, closed my eyes, and, lying back on the table, tried to cover up with the completely useless paper gown they leave for you. First came the exhale—the big exhale—and then the silent tears started to flow out of the corners of my eyes, dripping into my ears. There was no stopping those tears flooding out, wet and hot. I was starting to get a penetrating, strong message that I did not belong here. It was as if I was being guided in a dream-like state. I reached for the chair with my belongings on it, put my clothes back on with the agility and grace of an ostrich on Valium, and fled, making no attempt to tell anyone that I was leaving. I jumped into my Jeep and went for a long ride in the desert. I felt a frisson of relief, like I had just broken out of prison, like I'd had a narrow escape. I wanted distance, I wanted open road, and I wanted to be alone.

I found my pull-off spot halfway to Mexico. The day was spent, and the moon was all the light I needed to cry my eyes out. I screamed at the sky, cursed my stupid life, and asked, "Why me?" I cried the deepest tears I could, and eventually lulled myself to sleep. There I lay, asleep in my Jeep with my face pointed up to the sky, exhausted. Then, up from the worlds of slumber, came a very different kind of dream. It was the most vivid dream I'd ever had. Time stood still and I can't be sure my soul was on this planet while I was in this dream, because I could understand in some way that I could also see myself back on Earth.

Something was fluttering and bobbing around me, and I squinted to
make out its form. It was a little cherub, completely mesmerizing and
so completely odd. I watched him sway all around me, checking in on
me, and dancing about. Then he said hello in my mind, as if he was not
sure I could see him, or that I understood. His hair was curly and sandy
blond, and he had a little gap between his front teeth. His skin was
tanned by the sun, as though he spent all his free time at the beach,
playing cherub games. He nodded at me. "Everything will turn out all
right," he seemed to say, and he sort of shrugged, smiled, and he was off
into the sky. I clearly remember waking up, so I knew it was a dream,
and I thought, "Wow, that was a message." It was the first of many
angel messages I have received in my life.

I didn't give the dream much more thought, nor did I understand that it was angel inspired. I crawled into the driver's seat, headed back to the lights of the city, and called my mom. She invited me home and I took the invitation. I proceeded through a difficult pregnancy, involving being bedridden for seven months. Nothing made me happier than getting off bed rest. The baby and I had plenty of time to bond. I found us an apartment, went back to my old job, and life seemed to be getting back to normal. It was just me and this little guy, hanging out, going through life. When I did laundry, I would often plop my baby into the laundry basket to keep him from running all over the place. Then I could take him from room to room while I put everything away. One day as I was finishing the crib with fresh clean sheets, I looked over at my son playing in the basket. Instantly, my stomach and my mind lurched back to the day in the desert almost two years earlier. I was transported out of my body to a space in time that seemed so long ago. I could totally feel and taste that moment in the desert. My son was the cherub but, like Pinocchio, he was also a real boy! I was so enthralled with his appearance in the dream because he had a unique look. And ever so slowly my son had grown into the exact image of the cherub in my dream. He had not been big enough until this very moment for me to see it. I let my shoulders down and exhaled very deeply, saying, "Okay, I guess you're here." I nodded my head, because now I understood so many things that flooded into my mind with no words. I knew I had a bigger role to play in this relationship, and that I was being asked to do something extra—it was as if I was to guide a

king. He was supposed to come to me. We are on a journey, we are
protected, and the angels are watching. I even snapped a picture
to commemorate the moment, and it's still one of my favorites.

Now, twenty years later, I can look back. That boy was beyond
difficult to raise, especially in his teen years, and we needed every
angel we could get to stand by and get him through. I've never met
another person whom I thought could have taken this boy on the path
he was supposed to be on, nor have I ever thought that another would
have been a better guide. His lessons and gifts are going to change the
course of his life, and many other people's lives. People have stopped
me all throughout his life, on the street, in airports, and in restaurants,
and asked me if I knew he was an old soul, an indigo child, or that he
was blessed. I let out a big deep breath, nod my head, smile, and I assure
them, "It's a crazy ride but I'm glad I took the job!" It has taken me so
very far from the small life I had imagined for myself that day back in
the toaster waffle bathroom.

Jenny says: Who knows what wonders Mickey's
son may perform in years to come? I do believe that our children
choose us and we choose them. This may be hard for people to
comprehend when we see such apparently dysfunctional families
in the world. But there is a meaning to everything. We all have
lessons to learn and experiences to endure in order for our soul,
or the souls of those we interact with, to progress. It's part of the
everlasting mystery of our lives. Mickey had strong confirmation
that she and no one else was meant to have this child, and I'm
sure all the reasons will become clear in time.

Steve's story:

Strength to Change

From childhood I'd had very low self-esteem. I can remember feeling the weight of the world on my shoulders at infant school, and although there were happy times, too, things never really improved from then. It's always been my desire to help people, and I'd decided to work for the emergency services by the time I was ten years old. At sixteen, I became a member of the British Red Cross, attending public events to carry out first-aid duties.

Then on January 8, 1989, a plane crashed near our local airport. Although I was not involved in the rescue work, I was part of a team from the Red Cross that went to a local hotel to care for the relatives of the injured and the missing. I still feel guilty that I could not reach out to these people and care for them as they should have been looked after. I felt so shell-shocked. For instance, I saw a mother and father having to identify their son by a blood-stained watch, and that was it—all they had left of him. Life carried on, but this and other occurrences festered in my head, eating away at me, burning doubt in my mind. Also, when I was a teenager, my father had attempted suicide, become addicted to painkillers, and subsequently had a nervous breakdown.

I'd met the love of my life in 1988 and we married five years later. The bad memories were still there but love dulled them. Our son was born eight years later, to add more love to our family. In 2003 I landed my dream job in the fire service, and things were on the up and up.

I excelled at my job and was soon promoted. I sometimes feel that this was the start of my downfall.

Not long after I was promoted, I was in charge of an incident that went wrong, and I could have quite easily killed the people whose safety I was supposed to ensure. Negative feelings started to resurface, and my mind filled with doubt about my ability, my life, and my very existence. I felt I was alone, not worth my wife's attention, and actually bad for her and my son. Things were breaking down rapidly. It felt like I was constantly angry with the whole world. My workload increased tenfold. At first this was a welcome distraction from my situation but, with an unsupportive manager, it soon started to add to my feelings. Then I committed the ultimate sin and had an affair. My low self-esteem made me feel that this was bound to happen. Needless to say, as all mistaken affairs do, it ended in catastrophe. It turned into a controling, abusive relationship that I couldn't end, and finally my wife found out. As you can imagine, she was devastated and I hit the lowest point ever, wanting to end my life.

I'd like to say that's when the angels saved me but it's not. They had been with me all the time. I just didn't know it. I think about it now and can recall the warming tingle on my left side at low points, and just dismissing it as twinges or pins and needles. My wife, amazingly, agreed to stay with me, even though I'd treated her so badly. We sought counseling to help us through the tough times. We also sought the help of a spiritualist church, and one of the readings I was given said an angel was looking over me and constantly covering me with its wings. This had such a positive effect on me, knowing that I was being cared for no matter how bad times were or would be. Through our attendance at the church I am developing my healing and psychic abilities by working with the angels, which has brought about the most positive feeling I can imagine. I'm no longer the angry person I once was. The joy I now have is indescribable, and the calmness in my life is amazing. I know that there is still suffering in this world of ours but I feel it's my purpose, in my small section of the globe at least, to offer to bring peace and hope to those who seek it. And the best bit is knowing that I have angels surrounding me, and I still have my own earth angel, too.

Jenny says:

Steve certainly did have some hard lessons to learn and tough experiences to endure, but now he's a different person, perhaps the person he was always meant to be. He shouldn't feel guilt about his earlier life, because he's been strong enough to learn and to allow himself to be changed. Now he can go on to achieve his real life's purpose.

Wendi's story:

Resourceful Angels

This happened to me about six years ago. I was married at the time, and my then husband had starting to hang around with a younger guy, Sam, who considered it okay to go out until the early hours of the morning and leave his girlfriend and baby at home most nights. Sam

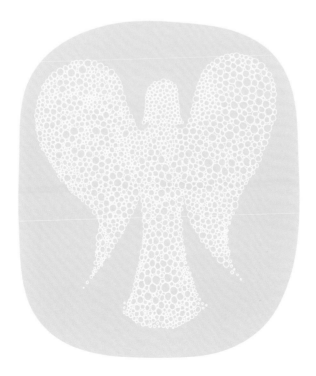

hung around with a group of people who needed to grow up quite a lot, and soon enough, my husband started doing the same. I tried to talk to him. I realized where it was heading, but he carried on behaving in the same way. As I'd guessed, he'd met a young girl, Rachel, and had been unfaithful to me. It completely shattered my world and our children's world, too. Although we stayed together, of course I found it so hard to trust him again, and there was a great strain on the relationship. I got to a point where I knew I needed help with the emotions I was feeling, and I'll quote you word for word from my journal what happened one day when I was in the bathtub:

On one hand I held Sam and all the emotion relating to him and the effect it had on me and my marriage. On the other hand I held Rachel and the group of people in general, and all the emotion that went with that. I wanted to release it all up to the angels, together with all the hurt and the pain their actions had caused. I didn't want it any more; I wanted to be able to release it, no negativity any more, only positivity. But my hands were shut tight around the pain and I felt I couldn't let go. Then I felt my hands slowly loosening. I shut my eyes, asking the angels to send me the confidence to let go, and they did! My hands flew open and everything was released up to

them. I asked them if they would deal with it all, and I felt emotional that they would help me in this way. I looked down at the bathwater in front of me and saw the shape of an angel made out of the remainder of the bubbles in the bath!

I'll never forget that experience. My husband and I stayed together for a few years after that, because I had more strength, but he did the same thing again, so I divorced him. Since then the angels have worked their magic and I met a wonderful man, my true soul mate, whom I know I'll be with for ever and ever.

Another experience I had was a couple of years ago at the Guildhall in Southampton when my sister and I went to see psychic Tony Stockwell. About halfway through the evening, a large pure white feather floated down from the ceiling and landed toward the middle of the room. We were indoors and there were no windows open. This feather just floated down and landed on someone as though it was the most natural thing in the world. I turned to my sister open-mouthed, and my eyes met hers. She was also open-mouthed. Nobody else in the room noticed it, not even those seated just where it landed. Amazing!

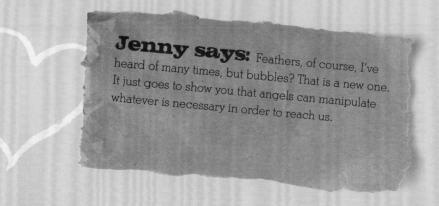

Jenny says: Feathers, of course, I've heard of many times, but bubbles? That is a new one. It just goes to show you that angels can manipulate whatever is necessary in order to reach us.

CHAPTER 8

CHILDREN AND ANGELS

Children and angels—they are the perfect combination of innocence, trust, and the divine miracle. If only we could all be like children and accept that angels are close to us as an everyday fact, how much happier we'd all be. Given good circumstances, all children start off with innate joy and the perfect state of energy. This means they talk to angels on a regular basis every day. It's a pity, but part of our challenge of being here on Earth is that we lose this ability and have to regain it. Some of these stories are quite old, and I was delighted to receive them and have it confirmed to me that angels never change.

Bea's story:

A Beautiful Moment

When I was about eight years old, I used to have to go to Sunday school. One Sunday morning we'd been talking about how saying prayers can be like mailing beautiful letters to God. We'd talked about how to be good, why it was important, and what a beautiful thing it was to make others happy in any way we could, without asking for thanks but simply because we were able to do it. I'd walked home brooding on this, and on the way picked a big bunch of wildflowers, which I divided up into little posies, leaving one on the doorstep of all the moms I knew. I had no intention of being seen, but one lady opened the door suddenly as I was closing the gate, and called, "Thank you!" after me. I remember seeing her smile, and then I shot off home.

What happened next is something I didn't share with anyone for many years. For one thing, I didn't have the language to express myself satisfactorily. I sat on the edge of my bed—I can recall this as if it was yesterday—and looked out of the window. "Is this how it feels to be good?" I said, either aloud or to myself, I don't know which. At that moment, a sensation came over me that now I would describe as pure love. Someone was next to me, and all around me, transforming the space where I was. Everything was still there in front of my eyes, but invisible at the same time, and within those seconds, or minutes—I have no idea of the time frame—all I felt was total love. I was touched by an angel who answered my question with unconditional love.

Some years later my dad asked me about it. "Well, was it the kind of amazing feeling you get when you look over a beautiful landscape?" I knew how that felt, and it was lovely, but it wasn't like that. This was "out of this world," and a million times better than any other feeling in my experience. I've willed that feeling to come back, over the years, sometimes even wishing it hadn't happened only at such a young age. To have felt it then was a blessing but once you've had it, do you want that feeling back! It was simply one of the most beautiful moments of my life—just me, and God, and the angel who'd heard me.

Cathryn's story:

Saved by an Angel

I'm a forty-eight-year-old journalist living in Parkdale, Oregon, in the beautiful Pacific Northwest region of America. When I was about three or four years old, I met a "nice lady," who told me that the honeybees I was "playing with" in a clover patch at Easter time were dangerous. It turns out I was allergic to the sting. She very likely saved my life that day, and has probably done so countless times since! She explained that she'd be with me always and that I'd hear her voice anytime I needed her, and that I would recognize her at the moment of my death. Even at such a young age, I understood very clearly that I will survive my death and that there is a life beyond the one I am living now. I remember being able to see her then, although now I mostly experience her as sound and a kind of

Jenny says: I loved these stories for two reasons. One is that although the events weren't world-shaking, they changed the writers for ever. The other is that they clearly demonstrate how children just accept this kind of thing, and don't find such happenings extraordinary, so, for me, proving their veracity. A child would find no reason to invent stories like these. It's only later, when we start to have pre-conceived ideas about angels and the world in general, that we start to question what we feel.

pressure/presence rather than seeing her as a physical manifestation. It turns out that my brother and sister also regularly interface with otherworldly beings—angels and those who have been embodied and have departed this life.

Follow the child

I always advise parents never to make fun of their children's experiences, no matter how laughable they might seem to cynical adults, but to encourage them to retain their intuitive acceptance of supernatural events into adulthood. Not only will they be happier, but they will also enrich the lives of those around them. Children see the truth, honestly and without question or judgment, unlike adults. We, sadly, are changed by parents, peers, teachers, friends, and family, who, while meaning well, only drive us away from our natural, spiritual, and intuitive path. They want us to fit, but we're not geometric shapes, and we shouldn't be made to change to suit society. That way, just as if bits of us have been chopped off to make us fit our boxes, we lose track of who we really are and why we're here, and we become stuck on a merry-go-round of cares and woes, instead of retaining our childlike sense of magic and the joy of being ourselves. Children can talk to angels just by asking, because it's natural to them, so nurture this ability in your child and you'll be doing a wonderful service for humanity, for your child is the future of the world.

Hazel's story:

Warning Voice

I was told this story recently, although it's actually years old. My cousin Tracy, who lives in Lancashire, came to Australia for a holiday in 1985 when she was fifteen. We took her and her parents to Phillip Island, a popular tourist attraction, to see the penguins. Tracy, being a bit of a tomboy, went off by herself and started running madly over the sand dunes, leaping and jumping in the sand. At some point she decided to run and take a jump off the dunes, but just before she reached the edge something shouted at her to stop. She pulled up and went forward more cautiously to look over the edge, still thinking it was just a sand dune. It wasn't, it was a cliff. If she hadn't heeded the warning and stopped running, she'd have jumped to her death, because what she had not seen was that the cliff fell away on the other side and she would have fallen fifty feet or more. I told her I believed her guardian angel had instructed her to stop that day, because none of the family was anywhere near her.

Cora's story:

Follow the Light

When I was about eight years old, our whole family went camping in a forest. I don't remember where it was, but I do know that I got lost. I'll never forget it. I'd wandered down a trail that looked easy to follow, and I kept thinking I'd just go along to the next corner to see what was there and then go back. As a child, I was easily distracted and I went farther and farther, attracted by interestingly shaped trees and

intriguing turns in the path. By the time I did turn back, the path had changed. What had seemed like just one path to me, now had lots of branches going off to the sides. I felt scared, but tried not to panic. I shouted for my parents, but all I could hear was the sounds of animals and birds. I tried path after path but couldn't find any that looked familiar. I didn't know it but we reckoned later that I had gone about two miles from our camp. I still don't know how that happened, and I'm eighty-three years old now.

Eventually, it began to get dark, and the birds changed to bats, which frightened me. I could hear owls screeching, and something yipping and crying out. That's when he came along. I wasn't a bit afraid, even though I'd been warned by my parents never to talk to strange men. He was sort of glowing and white, so bright that I couldn't see his face. I knew that he wanted me to follow him, so I did, and he led me for some distance. It was quite dark, but I could always see his glow. About an hour later I suddenly found myself stumbling back into our camp, and the man vanished. Amazingly, my parents were both standing there, looking right at me, as if they were expecting me to appear. After the hugs and kisses and phone calls to call off the search party, they told me they'd been looking at a bright light they could see through the trees, and then it went out, and there I was!

Jenny says: Cora was clearly a child who should never have been lost. The fact that she can recall such detail after nearly eighty years proves what an impact the escapade had on her. It would be interesting to sit down with her and discover what she's done in her life, because she was obviously saved for an important reason.

Larry's story:

Equine Angel of Mercy

This is a story about my grandmother, Flora, which has been handed down in the family as true and never to be forgotten. In 1890, Joachim Martens farmed a plot in Western Pennsylvania. It reminded him of the home he'd left behind in Germany many years previously, although this shale-ridden land was more reluctant to yield harvest. Joachim's daughter Flora, going on four years old and the light of his life, helped him on the farm. She would lift a piece of shale, drop a kernel of corn on the ground, put the shale back, and Joachim would pour a dipper of water over it. He would take a long step and point at another piece of shale, and so the process would go on.

There were many tasks little Flora could not do. She could feed the chickens and gather the eggs, but she could not toss hay from the loft or milk the cows. And she could not help make hay. Only one piece of land on the farm was suitable for hay making, at the top of a steep hill

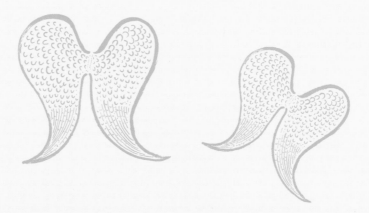
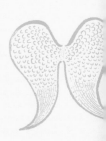

above the barn. When the hay was ready, it would be brought down to the barn on a wagon pulled by two horses, although on that steep gradient, the task had more to do with holding the wagon back than pulling it. Joachim would have to pull hard on the hand brake and on the reins to keep the wagon from running away. Only by sheer effort and skillful driving could he get the wagon to the barn and stop it on the threshing floor for unloading.

Flora had been warned not to play on the threshing floor during haying. But what does a three-year-old girl, going on four, know of danger? So, one day she was playing on the threshing floor just as Joachim was fighting to keep his hay wagon from running away. As he turned to enter the barn, he saw his beloved daughter. In his mind's eye, he saw her trampled by horses' hooves. He saw her fragile body sliced in half by the iron-rimmed wheels.

He cried out, and yanked harder on the reins. One of the team, an old gray horse named Bruce, took the bit in his teeth at this perilous moment. "I'll kill that beast!" thought Joachim as he tugged fruitlessly on the reins. Just as the horses reached Flora, Bruce suddenly released the bit he'd been fighting against. He opened his mouth, reached down, and grasped Flora's dress in his teeth. When the wagon stopped, Bruce gently lowered Flora to the floor.

When was the last time you saw an angel as a horse? The Martens family certainly thought of Bruce as an angel of mercy. And Joachim didn't kill him.

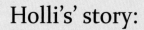

Holli's' story:

Divine Guidance

When my daughter was just four years old, we were at the pool, and I watched in horror as she started to climb up a high-dive ladder and slipped off it before I could get to her. She fell, not into the water, but onto the slab of concrete at the base of the board. I feared the worst, but the way she fell seemed to defy physics. There was no possible human way she could have landed on her back, but she did. She should have hit every step and bounced down the ladder. She should have broken every bone in her body. She was wearing a life jacket, which absorbed the fall somewhat, but the moment I saw that she was miraculously unharmed, I believed that an angel had guided her down. My father is deceased, and at that moment I felt his presence. There is no doubt in my mind. Then about ten years ago I was riding my bike in the city of Chicago when a truck made a right turn and hit me. I thought I would be crushed for sure, but again, miraculously, I was pushed off my bicycle sideways, unharmed. I really should have been squished. My body defied gravity in the way I was able to pop off my bike and not be hurt. I believe I was divinely guided. Again, I have no doubt that angels were at work.

Paulie's story:

Misty Presence

I remember it like it was yesterday, even though I'm nineteen now and I was only ten when it happened. My little brother Benny was in hospital suffering from meningitis, and even though I was only young, I knew my mom and dad expected him to die. One evening, as I was watching Benny while they went for a break, and praying to God, a white mist appeared right over his head. It got quite thick and I was scared, so I went to fetch a nurse, but by the time we arrived back the mist had gone. She said maybe it was condensation and went back to her post. I sat down again and after a while the mist came back. It took on a shape, like a woman with big wings. My heart jumped and I thought, he's going to make it. When my mom and dad came back, I told them not to worry, Benny has an angel, and he's going to be all right. I thought this would make Mom feel better but it scared her. She thought the angel, if there really was one, had come to take him to heaven. I didn't think that was right.

The doctor kept popping in all that night, and I think he was just waiting for Benny to die, but he didn't, and by morning they were all talking about miracles. I know it was a miracle, because I saw it!

Jenny says:

This is a classic example of how a child can accept angelic help easily, naturally, and without question, whereas an adult may be frightened by it. It's such a shame that we lose our ability to accept wondrous events at face value.

Simone's story:

Reassuring Visit

When my cousin Christy and I were both aged about seven, she was in hospital. I don't remember her being sick, but I do remember being told that she was going to live in heaven with her mom, who had died four years previously. I just accepted this, like children do sometimes, but Christy didn't really remember her mom and I worried whether Christy's mom would know her after all this time. I figured, though, they probably would know each other.

I used to play with Christy a lot. We had shared a big Victorian-style doll's house that two aunties had bought for us. When she did pass, I was a bit lonely. I'd play with the doll's house, thinking how nice it used to be when Christy was there. One day, I was wondering whether I'd be scared when it was my time to die, and a light suddenly appeared in the doll's house. It grew bigger until it came into the room. I wasn't

scared, just caught by wonder. The light grew into an angel, with wings and a halo, and she was leading Christy by the hand. My cousin just stood there, glowing in the angel's light, and she smiled at me. Then she and the angel faded away.

Find your inner child

If you'd like to rekindle some of that childhood wonder, there is something you can try. We have all had moments in our childhood that meant a lot to us or have affected us deeply in some way. They can be moments when we felt great love and pride being extended to us by someone else, or moments of shame and despair. Whether it was a positive or negative moment, the strategy is the same up to a point.

✳ Sit somewhere comfortable at a time when you won't be disturbed, and close your eyes.

✳ Recall whatever incident you feel was most pivotal, and replay it in your mind. Re-create the moment and the emotions you felt at the time.

✳ Calm your breathing and allow your adult mind to flow back to that time, seeing yourself as the child caught in that moment.

✳ Observe, and imagine the emotions the child is going through.

✳ Open your arms and your heart and draw the child back into your adult body. Feel the emotions, good or bad, course through you. If the emotions were good, allow them to light you up with joy by allowing yourself to be that child again. If the emotions were bad, hold the child close, say that your love is unconditional, and that you are there to take away the hurt.

✳ Take a few moments to experience the reunion and, when you're ready, open your eyes and return to the current time and place.

✳ This is a form of soul regeneration and its wonderful, pure energy will draw flights of angels toward you. Don't let this moment go, but try to think of it as many times a day as you can. The closer you are to your inner child, the closer you are to your angels.

CHAPTER 9
ANIMALS AND ANGELS

At the beginning of this book I mentioned that animals can sometimes be used as angel messengers but, actually, I would go further than that. I feel that animals are more spiritual than humans. All their intuitive and instinctual powers remain totally intact, while we lost ours long ago. Once, humans could smell water from miles away, and they knew what roots and berries to eat for medicinal purposes—talents that animals still possess. Humans have almost no connection to nature and the planet nowadays, but animals are completely in tune with both. Humans act in ways that they know and understand will harm other people, whereas animals act only out of instinct and for their own survival. Humans behave cruelly, in the name of fun or sport, and have set themselves up as the rightful deciders of which creatures should live and which should die. Humans deliberately say hurtful things in order to bring someone else down. Animals never deliberately use cruelty against others, and what may sometimes seem like cruelty to us is just the operation of the survival instinct. The difference is in the intent. Humans discriminate against others because their skin is a different color or they believe in different things, whereas to animals we are all equal and all treated purely on the basis of our own behavior.

So, taking all this into account, it's no surprise to me that animals are able to see spirits quite often, and also bring messages from angels. Sometimes they even appear to hold a divine energy, either permanently or temporarily, in order to bring angelic help to us.

Mykey's story:

Psychic Horses

I'm a horseback rider and handler, and one of the horses I look after is called Milargo, a beautiful black Friesian. One day at a show, I was alone with Milargo, happily grooming him while listening to the radio, when I accidentally banged my head on a rail and blacked out. I must have fallen against the horse because when I came round, he was holding me up against his body—and most amazingly, he was using his

nose to splash me with water from his bucket. I couldn't get my balance, so I untied him and held onto his side while I made my way over to some shade where I was able to sit down. He stood over me, protectively. I kept going under and he would nudge me with his nose to wake me up.

Later on I was told that I'd had an epileptic seizure. Milargo certainly did the best he possibly could for me. I've known him since I was a baby and believe he was my angel that day. Who knows what would have happened if he hadn't kept me against him or had spooked when I fell against him.

Eight months later I was working with another horse, Glorious Way. I was at a show with him in a jumping class. We went into the ring and he suddenly started hesitating in the corners. Our first jump was perfect, but then he stopped and refused to jump. I thought he was in a mood and being stubborn. I don't remember exactly what happened next, besides the fact that I'd had a seizure. I came round lying on Glorious Way's neck. He wouldn't let anyone touch me. It was unlike him to bite but he threatened anyone who tried to touch me. He waited until he could feel I had my balance back and then he started walking toward the gates. As I slipped off he used his neck to support me and keep me on my feet.

Jenny says: Dogs and cats are being used more and more to sense and track certain diseases, such as cancer, diabetes, and epilepsy, but I never before heard of a horse being able to do so. With dogs and cats, scientists have put it down to changes in scent, rather than any psychic ability. However, that doesn't explain the behavior of these two horses. A horse's sense of smell is not the same as a dog's or a cat's, and even if it was, these horses didn't sniff Mykey.

Gail's's story:

Connected for Ever

I believe the animal soul is possibly even more profound and grounded than the human soul. About three years ago, my father, who had passed some fifteen years earlier, came to me in a vision, or an awake-type of dream, in a time of intense stress and duress in my life. He told me that things would be okay, but what made it real was that he also said, "Lucky watches out for you, too." Lucky was our family dog, a tricolored collie who had been gone since I was sixteen. What is interesting is that, for a moment, I felt her beside me. I could smell her, feel her fur, and I could sense the comfort that my father and Lucky found in each other after death. I'd never had an experience before or after that was so profound. I think that when you connect with an animal's soul, you're connected for ever. They wait for you in the next life, just like your family.

Jenny says:

It's very comforting to think that, once they pass over, our loved ones meet with others we've known and people they have loved. To understand that they also meet the pets that we have loved is better still.

Terry's story:

A Mighty Protector

Peanuts was part Australian shepherd dog and part border collie, a healthy three-pound ball of white fluff when my father found her wandering on the side of a busy highway outside Medford, Oregon, and took her home. I was born four months later and more or less became the newest addition and responsibility in Peanuts's ever-expanding world. Besides her usual duties of annoying the dairy cattle, herding the barn cats and the itinerant yard chicken, she now had her very own boy to raise, and she took this duty very seriously. She was there during every feed, as well as every time I cried. She steadied me during my first steps, volunteering to be my climbing device, and my cushion when I fell. She watched by my bed through every childhood illness and malady.

Over the years, she became our family's emotional barometer. She always knew when someone was sick, or sad, or even just lonely. She would make the rounds every night, stopping next to or in front of everyone's chair. Once she was acknowledged, she was content, and would move on. On that rare occasion when she was ignored, she would force her face into the hand of the person in question until she was given a big hug and a scratch behind both ears. Ensuring that her family was well and content was her lot in life, and she accomplished it with perfection.

For over sixteen years she was more than a pet. She was my best friend and confidante. I found I could tell her things I couldn't tell my family or friends. When I needed her the most, she stayed by my side day and night. She was there while I struggled to learn how to walk again after polio. She listened when I told her about the first time a girl broke my heart. She rejoiced in my successes as well as comforting me after each and every failure. It was an incomprehensible loss the day she died. As children we're told that heaven awaits a person's soul, and death is little more than part of the circle of life. But we're never told what becomes of one of our greatest loves, the one that has never asked for anything but love from us while giving us unconditional love in return. Don't our pets' souls deserve the same happiness as ours are promised? You might think that this story ends here. Peanuts lived and Peanuts died, but is that the end?

Thirty years after Peanuts died, my grandfather lay on his deathbed, being eaten from the inside by a cancer for which there was no cure. I kept my vigil by his bedside, and late one night I administered a dose of morphine to ease his pain. His temperature had spiked and he was becoming agitated, when all of a sudden an unusual calm came over him. His right arm lay uncovered on the side of the bed. I watched as his hand bumped into the air once and then once again. It settled almost four inches above the mattress. Slowly, his hand began to move as if stroking the soft fur of a familiar face. Early the next morning, his hand settled slowly to the bed, and my grandfather took his last breath. As I sat there numbed with grief, I felt hot breath and the cold damp nose that was all too familiar, as the weight of Peanuts's head lay gently in my lap. When I didn't respond, she poked her nose into the palm of my hand gently but insistently, sliding it on top of the soft fur of her forehead. I instantly understood her purpose and that everything that was promised during our life had come to pass. I don't believe that the pets we love so dearly ever leave us. They're always there when we need them, sharing their unbridled love with us during those moments when we need it most.

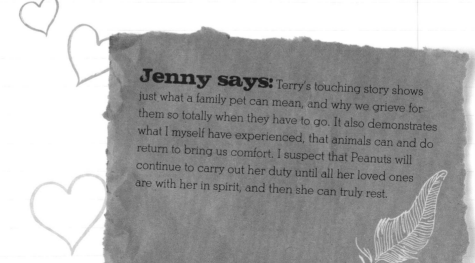

Jenny says: Terry's touching story shows just what a family pet can mean, and why we grieve for them so totally when they have to go. It also demonstrates what I myself have experienced, that animals can and do return to bring us comfort. I suspect that Peanuts will continue to carry out her duty until all her loved ones are with her in spirit, and then she can truly rest.

Maureen's story:

Compassionate Pet

For the last two weeks I have been having an experience that I cannot really understand and would like to share. For almost fourteen years I had a lovely Polish sheepdog, Doerak, who was my soul mate. Wherever I went, there was my dog. Sadly, in November 2010 I had to take the most difficult decision to have him gently put to sleep. He was very sick and could not possibly recover. It was my obligation to let him go so that he didn't suffer. The vet came to my home and it was time for Doerak to go to the place behind the rainbow. I could see in his eyes that it was time for him to leave me.

The house was very empty without him, so much so that I had to get a new puppy, who is now eight months old. Benji came to my home in April 2011. For the first three months he grew up with my old cat Whiskey, who died in June. Whiskey was a lovely, friendly cat, who knew three of my dogs—Pipo, Doerak, and the puppy Benji.

On an old table in the corner of my bedroom are some pictures of my family, and also of Doerak and Whiskey with the urns containing their ashes. Benji had never shown any interest in them until recently. I was in the sitting room and could hear Benji "talking" in a special way in my bedroom. He wasn't barking or whining for attention; no, it was some special conversation. I went to see what was happening, and he was sitting beside the table with his head lifted up in the direction of the urns, focused on one point and making the "talking" noise. I could not distract him from it because he was so intent. This has been going on for almost two weeks. It's not every day and not always at the same time.

Is it possible that either Doerak or Whiskey, or both, are now talking to Benji? Or perhaps my mother is saying something through Doerak? During her illness she formed a close bond with my Doerak, and on the evening she almost suffocated, Doerak was in a total panic for a few hours beforehand, so much so that it looked like he was suffocating—I thought that maybe someone had given him a bone, which was not the case—and he refused to enter my mother's room. He was standing in the doorway when he panicked. I think he already knew that when the night came, my mother would fall into a coma.

Jenny says: Maureen's story of a deceased pet communicating with a living one is unusual. What I think is happening here is that the two dogs are discussing whether Maureen is ever going to recover from the loss of Doerak, and that perhaps Benji might allow the other dog's soul to join him in his body so that his owner can feel him close to her again. I've heard of many instances of this "joining" taking place.

Vivienne's story:

Okay Cats

Both my cats came back to me after they'd died. I loved those cats and really missed them. Some six months after Tom died I found a line of orange paw marks on my bedroom windowsill, although I had no cat at the time. I cleaned them off, which I regretted afterward, and a week later found two more paw marks under a photo of Tom on the same windowsill. I know it was him come to say he was okay.

My next cat, Sooty, lived to be sixteen and then developed an illness and had to be put down. This was in 2005. His habit was to sit by the radiator outside my office at home when I was working, and breathe heavily in an asthmatic sort of way to announce his presence. He once really frightened my assistant with the heavy breathing because she thought someone had broken into the house. About six months after Sooty died, I was on the phone in the office when loud breathing started up in the hall. I could hear it all through the phone call. When I had finished my call, I sat listening for a bit and then opened the office door. The breathing stopped and there was nothing to see. Again, I knew it was Sooty coming by to say that he was okay.

Jenny says:

Animals may leave little signs when they come back to visit, just as human spirits may do, and sometimes they just pop back to reassure us that they're all right, as Vivienne discovered with Tom and Sooty.

Sarah's story:

Harry, My Angel

We had two pet rabbits and when we got home from vacation one Friday, they both seemed fine. The next day, however, it was a different story. My rabbit, Harry, was a little bit off his food in the morning, so I picked some dandelions for him; he seemed to like them and perked up a little. However, when I went back out to check on him a little while later, he was not well at all. He was very quiet and had lain right at the back of his run. I took him into the house and wrapped him in some towels and we sat together for a while. I could feel that he was slowly drifting away and I asked him if he wanted to stay here with me or if I should take him to the vet. I felt as if he told me he wanted to stay with me, so we sat together for a while longer and then I had a

No fear

When my beloved dog Ace was alive, she was frightened of thunderstorms right up until her later years, when her hearing went. The first time we had a storm after she'd died, we distinctly heard her paw-steps coming up the stairs and into the bedroom. She jumped onto the bed, huffed into each of our faces, and then after turning a few circles on top of the duvet, settled in between our legs, dragging the cover with her as she lowered herself down. I think it was her way of telling me that, although she was fit and well again in spirit and her hearing was restored, I needn't worry because she was no longer afraid of the storms.

strong feeling that he wanted to be on his own, so I took him to his hutch and wrapped him up in a blanket and tucked him in the hay. I said my goodbyes to him and when I checked on him after about 30 minutes, he had passed away. I asked for the angels to take his spirit and make sure he was okay, and when I looked up into the sky, I saw a cloud in the shape of a jumping rabbit, which slowly faded away. I felt instantly that he was happy and at peace. I also felt that he had waited for me to come home from vacation and I was so grateful for that. About an hour later my neighbor's daughter (whom I hadn't seen for a few weeks) knocked on my door and handed me a bracelet with a rabbit on. She said she had made it and thought of me. Although I was upset at Harry passing, it was also an amazing day for me. If I didn't believe before, I certainly do now! Thank you, Harry, my Angel, and thank you to all angels for bringing me this wonderful sign.

Contact your pet

If you've lost pets and would like some signs from them, try the following.

✳ Sit in your pet's favorite place, perhaps with his/her favorite toy.

✳ Close your eyes and open your mind.

✳ Ask your pet to make a sound, either with his/her toy or breath. If you have other pets, open your eyes and watch their behavior, because that will probably tell you when your pet in spirit is near.

✳ Ask your angels to help your pet to come through. The love we have for our pets and they have for us is truly unconditional and unselfish, and nothing can draw in angels more than this emotion.

Paul's story:

Lucky Jim

I work for an animal charity in the US that helps the homeless feed their pets, usually dogs. My job is to drive around collecting leftovers from restaurants and other places, and then leave the food at various places where we know the homeless hang out. One night I stopped at one of my usual places and was surprised to see one of my "regular's" dogs, waiting by himself. His owner, Jim, had always been with him before. The dog was a mixed breed called Sandy, and I thought it was his lucky night, as, unusually, a restaurant I had called in at had given me some nice leftover roast chicken. But Sandy wouldn't touch it. He just started barking at me and turning to leave, then turning back and barking again. Eventually, I used my brains and followed him. He set off at a lope and led me about half a mile through streets and alleyways until we came across Jim. Unable to move, he'd fallen and broken his ankle. How on earth Sandy had the intelligence to come to the feeding place and wait for me, I will never know. Or maybe he was led there by some other force?

As the crow flies

A friend was attending the funeral of a friend of hers. The lady who'd died had been a healer of animals and had said that she would use crows, her favorite birds, to send a message that all was well. After the service, when all the mourners were standing outside in the churchyard, the sky darkened. Looking up, the mourners were astounded to see that hundreds of crows were flying at a low level over the graves. The birds completed three circles and then flew away. No one was left in any doubt that their friend had spoken.

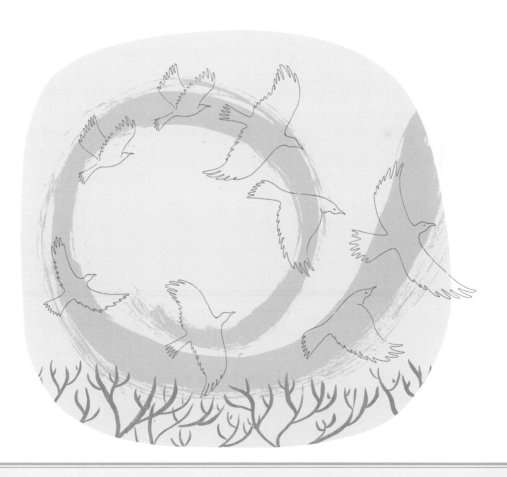

CHAPTER 10

HOW DO YOU CONNECT TO YOUR ANGELS?

Now you've read the stories, and maybe tried some of the snippets of advice that come with them, you may feel you want more instruction on how to get closer to your own angels. Most people, when asked about this, begin by mentioning your energy state, which is right, because angels live in a different dimension from the one we inhabit. They exist at a much higher rate of vibration than we do, putting them out of our reach for most of the time. Changing your energy is the most commonly accepted way to meet your angels on middle ground. As humans, we will never achieve exactly the same vibrational or energy levels as angels, otherwise we would become angels, but filling yourself with only positive thoughts will speed up your vibration and allow you to get halfway there, which is enough to form a connection.

Think positive

It's been my experience that some people just can't banish negative thoughts. Many find it impossible to switch off enough to reach a meditative state. Their heads are so full of everyday problems, perhaps sickness and pain, or perhaps financial or even mental issues, that the right, intuitive side of the brain has no chance against the left, logical side. No sooner do they start to drift off into whatever lovely scenario they've chosen to help them, than some little logical thought about a nagging problem snaps them back to the "real" world. So what are these people to do?

Having only positive energy involves having only positive thoughts and saying only positive things. This means no reading newspapers and no watching television news, because they inevitably involve negative events. People who are good at thinking only positive thoughts have come to realize that the news media hype up events, especially negative ones, in order to sell their product and, sadly, it works. They stir up one fearful scenario after another, whether it be an impending flu epidemic, financial crisis, or another looming war. Yet the more people refuse to be drawn into a scenario, the less likely it is to happen, and often if you shut yourself off from the media for a couple of weeks, you'll find the looming scenario has been forgotten and replaced by another one. Sadly, not enough people do ignore such information. We're only human after all. But those people who do take notice miss a fundamental truth—saying it, discussing it, thinking about it actually makes it happen. Unfortunately, it isn't possible to change the mind-state of everyone on the planet, so bad things keep happening.

Aids to relaxation

If you can't manage a meditation by yourself, another way to try to connect with your angels is with hypnosis. There are many good therapists around who can help you with this, and I have a worldwide list on my website. Hypnosis induces a state of total relaxation, which is often the hard part, and enables you and the therapist to communicate directly with your subconscious. Once you are in this

state, the therapist should be able to put you in touch with your angels, if you've specified that's what you want to do. The only drawback with this is that it doesn't work for everyone, and can be very expensive. One way around this is to use a meditation CD, but if you already find meditating difficult, then for several attempts, at least, all you will achieve is a relaxed-enough state to put you to sleep. This sort of relaxation is undoubtedly good for you, but it doesn't necessarily enable you to remain aware as you travel into your own subconscious. You're more likely to be in a deep sleep before you have a chance to think about it. Meditation CDs can work eventually, though, and at least you only have to pay for them once!

Help yourself

I am often sent stories by people who have received angelic help while they were in danger or in stressful situations, and since they can't possibly have been meditating or totally calm at the time, I faced a conundrum. How, I asked myself, could they have had the help they needed? So I came to realize that there must be another way, and this is it: "Give in order to receive." This is in the Bible in another form, and I heard it many times while I was growing up in Catholic schools, but I never really grasped its true significance until recent years. It's really very simple indeed. Whatever you want and need, you must give freely to others, because whatever you give out will come back to you, through angels, tenfold.

"Give in order to receive"

Security If you're afraid and yearn for angelic comfort, reassure or help someone in your everyday life. This can take the form of working for a thrift store, helping at a refuge for the homeless or battered women, counseling, or just simply being there for someone who is lost and upset.

Money If you're in financial trouble, it's no good asking angels to give you money—I've never known that to work. Understand, instead, that money has to flow, like a water course. If you moan and fret over every little thing you have to pay for, you effectively block the flow, and what can't flow out, can't flow in, either. So if you have a bill to pay, accept that you owe the money and hand it over with good grace. That way, the flow will become faster and smoother, and money will be able to come in.

Possessions If you long to have more possessions, then give some of those you have to others less fortunate than yourself. Give thoughtful little gifts whenever you can, and give kind words, too. Remember that these can bubble and skitter around in another's mind all day, and sometimes for the rest of a person's life. So be careful what you give with each word you speak.

Time In this day and age, we rarely have enough of this, and often ask for more, so it's surprising that giving works with time, too. Your time is the most precious gift you can give someone, but time is relative and can be stretched and contracted. We all know that if we're looking forward to something, time goes very slowly, but if we're dreading something, time flies. Don't be afraid to give your loved ones, and others in need, your time, because just like money it needs to flow. Give your time freely and happily, and your angel will stretch yours out for you and enable you to get more done than you thought you could in the time available.

Love If you long to meet your soul mate or just someone who will love you for yourself, then you must show and give love to others. Try not to hold grudges or say negative things about anyone or anything. If possible, forgive others and send them love, even if they've hurt you. Love will inevitably be drawn to love. It's irresistible, so once you have filled your being and your life with love and loving thoughts, you will find love coming back to you tenfold.

Anything you can think of that you'd like in your life may be treated in this way with a little imagination, and what is your imagination except your angels talking to you? If all this sounds too easy, sadly there is a catch. It's no good pretending. You have to mean it. Your intentions have to be perfect. It's no good giving if your motive is really personal gain. But, I promise you it is worth it. Angels really do want to help us. Yes, we all have lessons to learn and experiences to endure because we need our souls to progress, but angels can improve situations, even if they can't totally resolve them, and the more you find and accept their help, the more help you'll get. Angels don't like to see us hurt because they love us, and that is one thing you can be sure of. Whoever you are, wherever you live, whatever you do, angels will never stop loving you.

Loving angels

This emotion, love, really is the most powerful energy force in the universe. It's this love that enables angels to get through to us at all. When you consider that they live in a different dimension from us, it's obvious that they need something this powerful in order for us and them to be pulled close enough to communicate. That's why you never need to worry about whether you'll know if you have succeeded in connecting. The love you feel when close to an angel is simply euphoric. There's no mistaking it for anything else you've ever felt or are likely to feel. It totally supersedes all normal human emotions. I'm a firm believer that one day science will be able to prove the existence of angels. I watched a TV show recently in which it was explained that every atom on the planet and in the universe "talks" to every other atom. As science has discovered, no two atoms in the universe can exist simultaneously at exactly the same energy level. Energy levels are constantly fluctuating, so in order for this rule to be obeyed, the atoms must communicate with each other in some way, as if they know if the rule is going to be broken and can avoid it. Those of us who have had angelic communication don't need to wait for scientific evidence in order to believe, but it will be a great day for the world when all sceptics can become believers, too.

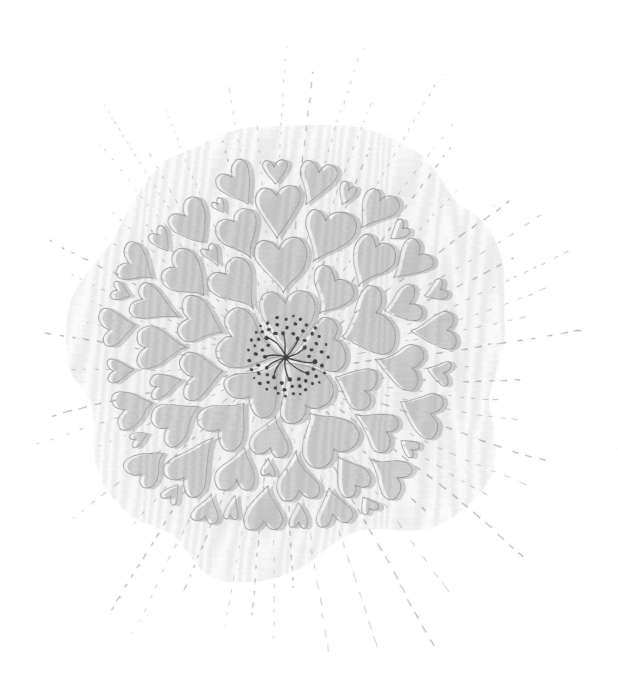

About the author

Jenny Smedley, DPLT (Diploma in Past Life Therapy), is a qualified past-life regressionist, author, television and radio presenter and guest, international columnist, and spiritual consultant, specializing in the subjects of past lives and angels. She lives with her husband, Tony, a spiritual healer, and her reincarnated "Springador" dog, KC, in beautiful Somerset, in the UK.

Her life was turned around by a vision from one of her past lives, in which she knew the man known today as Garth Brooks, the country music singer. Problems and issues related to that life were healed and resolved in seconds. By following the guidance she received from her angels, among other things, she became an award-winning songwriter overnight. Her angels enabled her to overcome a lifelong fear of flying to go to the US to meet Garth Brooks, so closing the circle.

For two years she hosted her own spiritual chat show on Taunton TV, and her guests included David Icke, Reg Presley, Uri Geller, and Diana Cooper. Jenny has appeared on many television shows in the UK, US, Ireland, and Australia, including, *The Big Breakfast*, *Kelly*, *Open House*, *The Heaven and Earth Show*, *Kilroy*, and *Jane Goldman Investigates*, as well as hundreds of radio shows, including *The Steve Wright Show* on BBC Radio 2, and *The Richard Bacon Show* on Five Live in the UK. She has also guested on the radio in the US, Australia, New Zealand, Iceland, Tasmania, the Caribbean, South Africa, and Spain.

Here are some comments that the national press have made about her:

"Unique rapport with the natural world" *Daily Express*
"A global phenomenon" *The Sunday Times Style* magazine
"World renowned for her ability to use angels to help people" *Daily Mail*

Jenny's website is: www.jennysmedley.com. She'd love to hear from you about your own angel experiences, so please get in touch by emailing her on: author@globalnet.co.uk and perhaps your story will be immortalized in another of her books. Please feel free to join Jenny on her Facebook page for some instant conversation with her and her friends: http://www.facebook.com/JennySmedleyAngelWhisperer

Previous books by Jenny Smedley

Past Life Angels

Past Life Meditation Audiobook

Souls Don't Lie

The Tree That Talked

How to Be Happy

Forever Faithful

Supernaturally True

Pets Have Souls Too

Angel Whispers

Soul Angels

Everyday Angels

Pets Are Forever

Angels Please Hear Me

A Year with the Angels

My Angel Diary 2012

My Angel Diary 2013

Resources

www.andtoto.org
www.watermewell.com
www.indigoangelbear.com
www.enchantedmakeovers.org
www.anexchangeoflove.com
www.animalcommunication.info

Suggested reading for animal lovers and those who believe that animals
have souls:
The Whale Whisperer Madeleine Walker (Findhorn Press)
An Exchange of Love Madeleine Walker (O-Books)

Index

Acknowledgments

This has been an exciting project for me as it's my first ever illustrated angel book, and so I'd like to thank everyone at CICO Books for giving me this opportunity, which I've really appreciated.

I'd like to thank all the wonderful people who have allowed me to use their stories, especially my friends on Facebook, who've been so generous and willing to share their experiences with me and with you.

My husband Tony has, as usual, been my reliable sounding board and constructive critic, so my thanks go to him too.

And most of all I'd really like to thank my angels, who have rewarded my faith in them by consistently bringing me these wonderful and new opportunities.